God, Hold Me While I Cry

How God Used Others To Bless Anna's Life

Don Dilmore

authorHOUSE®

AuthorHouse™
1663 Liberty Drive
Bloomington, IN 47403
www.authorhouse.com
Phone: 1-800-839-8640

First published by AuthorHouse   3/11/2011

ISBN: 978-1-4567-4501-1 (e)
ISBN: 978-1-4567-4503-5 (sc)

Library of Congress Control Number: 2011903622

Printed in the United States of America

"Let us hold unswervingly to the hope we profess, for He who promised is faithful."
Hebrews 10:23

This book is dedicated to all those who have suffered hardship, hoping that after you read Anna's story, you will know, without a doubt that if we will ask God to come into our lives, anything is possible. His love will overcome any handicap, hardship or disappointment.

Foreword

Over the past several years, I have become more and more interested in seeing how God works in our lives. It seems that God has crossed my path with several people who have had dramatic changes take place in their lives. In every one of those acquaintances, I have noticed that several people had a part in those changes.

For over fifty years, I have tried to be a faithful witness. I participated in Monday night visitations in various churches. I spent three weeks back in the bush in Tanzania, witnessing to people who had never heard the Word of God. My wife and I volunteered to spend two years working for the Canadian Southern Baptist Seminary, and during that time I pastored a church that started with fourteen members. We had great opportunities to share our witness.

In all of this time, there were many who accepted Christ. There were also many who did not. For a while, it bothered me when someone rejected the witness, but I began to realize that most of those who prayed to accept Jesus had others in their lives who had shared with them before I did. There had been rejection, but God's Spirit prevailed, and all who had witnessed to that person had a part in their salvation. I also saw some who made professions of faith with someone else leading them within a short period of time after I had shared with them. I soon learned that my job was to be a witness, not the judge or the jury. If I am faithful to witness, God's Spirit will be faithful to convict.

A little more than six years ago, a man called me and asked if I would write his life story. When I asked why he was calling on me, he said he had read the biography of Max Copeland, pastor for 43 years at First Baptist Church in Marble Falls, THE HILL COUNTRY PASTOR, THE MAN

WITH THE RED SOX. The caller said he liked the way I told the story and he wanted me to tell his story.

I was very apprehensive the first time I met with Wade Lackey. I couldn't imagine why he was asking me to write his life story. The day I met Wade he was at a Craft Show, selling bolo ties and arrowheads he had made with flint rock. Over the next few weeks I began to appreciate why he wanted his story told. It was almost an unbelievable story of being an alcoholic, a druggie, a drug pusher. His early life included stealing gasoline from neighboring farmers, breaking fish and game laws, committing adultery, burning all of his wife's clothes out in the yard. Then through the witness of several people, mainly his eight-year-old daughter, Wade became a Christian, passed the test for his GED, graduated from college and seminary, and pastored for almost thirty years.

When I submitted the manuscript to the publisher, they bar-coded it fiction. It was a story hard to believe. People still ask, after they read GOD WAS THERE ALL THE TIME, "Was all of that really true?"

I knew his story was hard to believe, but I was aware of several other similar stories that were difficult to believe. I already knew Dottie Compton. She had a similar story of God's loving hand, intervening into a life that seemed destined for tragedy. A TV evangelist was among those who witnessed to her. Her life moved from being an unwed mother living in a city park, to running one of the largest ministries to indigents and girls in trouble in our area.

I was a first-hand witness to our youngest daughter's bout with cancer when she was five years old. The head neuro-surgeon at Southwestern Medical School told us on the day before her fifth birthday, "Take her home and give her the biggest birthday party you can. She won't be here next year. Three years later four different doctors told us she could not live through the night. Several years later a doctor, who had laughed at me when I said we wanted to pray about an experimental treatment he wanted to use, told a nurse in my presence, "This was nothing a doctor or medicine did. God healed that little girl." He became a Christian sometime during that seven years, as a result of the testimony of many people.

I recently spoke at a meeting where Rocky Vasquez and Joe Dominguez also spoke. These two men spent years in prison, were members of gangs, one of them shot six times and stabbed twice. Then God intervened and today they both minister for Him.

A few weeks ago, on a Sunday morning, Anna Lybarger gave her testimony in church. It was another unbelievable story of how God worked for years in a young girl's life, when it seemed everything that could go wrong, did go wrong. This book is her story.

This is my point. There are miracles all around us. God is taking lives that have faced tragedy, abuse, sorrow; you name it, and turned those lives into useful servants for Him. In each situation, he has used people like you and me to share God's love with them. As you read Anna's story, be aware of the many people who in one way or another helped her to find God.

God has always been there to lift up the downtrodden and bring them into useful service. Peter, after he had denied Christ, the night of his crucifixion, was led by God a few weeks later to guide three thousand people to Christ at Pentecost. God spoke to Paul, who was on the road to Damascus to persecute Christians, and turned him into the greatest missionary our world has ever known. Both Peter and Paul, under the leadership of the Holy Spirit, contributed vital parts of the New Testament.

Today, I want to tell you Anna's story. You will find it hard to believe one woman has gone through so much tragedy, but she did. She always felt God was at her side, even from the time she was a small girl living in Germany, during the time the Nazi party controlled that country.

It is a true story, and I hope it will say to you, that no matter what kind of trials you have gone through or may be going through, if you will call on God, He will walk along side you and see you through. He will forgive any sin except the sin of disbelief. If you will trust in Him, He will always be there for you. There is no promise that you won't have problems, but God will help you through those times if you will trust in Him. He will always bring someone alongside you to help you.

Even before she knew much about God, Anna somehow sensed His presence in her life and she talked to Him as her Heavenly Father. Anna was FORGOTTEN BY EVERYONE BUT GOD, but in her despair, she cried out, GOD, HOLD ME WHILE I CRY, and He did.

Chapter One

Anna Rottenfusser was born in Munich, Germany February 24, 1939. Adolf Hitler had taken over the political reigns in Germany, with brutality, bestiality, and terror. Hitler's troops ruthlessly slaughtered Jews and many others in concentration camps. His troops rolled across Europe, conquering Austria, Czechoslovakia, Poland, Denmark, France and more.

The German army conscripted Anna's father, Johann Rottenfusser, and he was involved in the occupation of France in 1941. He came home for a short while, but when he refused to join the Nazi party, the military command quickly sent him to the Russian front. The family would not hear from him for many years. Anna's mother did discover where he was a short time later. They finally found out the Russian army captured him as a prisoner of war and held him there long after the war was over. They never heard directly from him. And, he would not see his youngest son until many years later.

Johanna, Anna's mother was left to care for seven children. The oldest daughter, named after her mother Johanna had been born in 1931; Helmut in 1934; Renate in 1935; Anna in 1939; Waltraud in 1941, Mathilde in 1942 and Hans in 1943. (These are approximates based on Anna's date of birth.) Anna says that Hans was definitely born after his dad went to the Russian front.

From theses dates, you can see that Anna's parents had seven children, the oldest being about twelve when their dad went to Russia. Anna told me her mother had six other children who had died before the war, but she doesn't know the details of their ages or the cause of death. Mama did not work, and the family had to live on a small government check.

Perhaps one of the strangest things about Anna's story is the fact that her mother never loved her. As we go forward, you will see this borne out by example. I asked Anna why her mother did not love her, and through the tears she told me she didn't know. She said, "I loved my mother and I wanted her to love me, but she never did. She never hugged me, or kissed me." Anna would see her siblings receive affection from their mother but it never happened with Anna. This fact continues until this day to haunt Anna. The lack of her mother's love, a father who left for army service when she was about four years old, and the terrible memories of bombing raids, witnessing atrocities, never knowing where the next meal was coming from, all have left Anna with memories she would just as soon erase from her mind.

She told me, "I still cannot watch war movies. It upsets me so much I have terrible dreams." For many years these dreams kept her from sleep, afraid of dreaming if she went back to sleep.

Raised in a Roman Catholic family in the 1940's and 50's, Anna went to Mass with her sisters, but she never saw a Bible, knew very little about God, but as one tragedy after another invaded her life, she always called out to God for assurance.

She told me, "I never really shared my past with my children or my husband. Maybe I was afraid to bring it all back. Deep in my heart I really tried to erase the past, but the scars and the hurts were still there. Many times they became so painful that I felt the same wounds open up over and over again. I was always a dreamer, perhaps to shut out the reality of the seven years we spent trying to survive the war in Germany. But I know now, dreams can become a reality if we keep on having faith in God."

Anna always seemed to have a sense of God. By the time she was nine, she and her sisters went to mass at the Roman Catholic Church, a twenty-five minute walk from their house. Their mother did not go with them, nor did their brothers. Even before that, Anna felt a relationship with God. When she started school, her teachers talked about religion and impressed her young mind. This was her first witness.

Anna's early years were years those of us in this country can only imagine. We have had the good fortune not to have to live through the death and destruction of bombing raids, a conquering army taking over our homes, having to scavenge in garbage dumps to get something to eat. These are memories a child can never forget.

Anna never really knew her father. She was quite young when he went into the army, and after the conquest of France, he was home for just a short while before the army sent him to the Russian front. Her father found it impossible to communicate with his family, so for many years they had no idea whether he was dead or alive, or exactly where he was.

So Mama Rottenfusser raised seven children, feeding and caring for them in a country that during Hitler's reign cared little for human life. Living in a very small apartment in Munich with almost no income, the family fought to exist. Anna said they had a small "blaupunkt" (radio) that played twenty-four hours a day. "We never turned it off," she told me. "The only information and news we received was on that radio. So we had to keep our ears open and listen constantly."

All of the children took turns listening. When they heard a siren sound, or the words "Achtung, Achtung, flieger alarm," the entire family had to be alerted. At night, this meant immediately waking up the others. Hurriedly dressing, they ran as quickly as possible to the "bunkers' (bomb shelters. There, they would often sit for hours, sometimes for days. Can you imagine the fear for a small child, running for your life over and over again, They had not asked for this war, but their lives were in constant danger, because an egocentric madman wanted to conquer the world.

Fortunately, there were some thoughtful people in those shelters, who tried to ease the fright of the children. Anna remembers a Mrs. Keller, who was always one of the first to the shelter. She brought cookies and sugar cubes for the children, and would often read them stories as they sat for hours waiting for the "all clear" signal so they could go back home.

Even then, things were not anywhere near normal. One child had the responsibility for listening to the radio. They could never play outside. They had to be sure they turned off all the lights by nine p.m.. The police ordered them to cover all windows with sheets and blankets. Young Johanna had the job of going outside each evening to check and see if there was any light showing from their apartment windows. You did what the government ordered you to do, because the Gestapo or the SS troopers patrolled the streets every night. If you are not familiar with the SS, they were formally known as the Waffen Schutztaffel. This was an elite force put together by Hitler. It was not a part of the army, but a private force of the Nazi party that started with a handful of Aryan men, but eventually became 38 divisions strong. Their symbol was a skull and crossbones and this should give you some idea of why children would be frightened enough to stay off the streets, and not play outside.

Anna's family would burn candles in the evening and would sit around the kitchen table whispering to each other, because they were told there was to be no noise that would reach out to the streets. Their radio, turned down to the lowest level was the most noise emanating from their apartment. Their fear of the Gestapo, a brutal police force, and the SS kept everyone on edge.

But the fear and the cause of bad dreams would seriously escalate in the weeks to come.

Chapter Two

One day, a neighbor, a man who had never spoken to them, came to visit. This was a surprise to the whole family, but particularly to Mama, who could have used a little help from her neighbors at times.

He didn't waste many words. "We want you to join the Nazi party," he told Mrs. Rottenfusser. "Things will be much easier for you if you do so. You will have a better life and more food for the children."

Mama was shocked at his request and his brusqueness, but it didn't take long for her to answer. She was strongly opposed to what the Nazi party was all about, and what they were doing. Their cruelty, their torture and killing of the Jews and others was common knowledge.

No!" was her reply, realizing she and the children would make some sacrifice by not going along. Then she added, "Where is my husband? Where have you taken him? You are a murderer. Murderer!" she screamed as she burst out crying. The neighbor tried once again to persuade her that things would be better if she would become a Nazi, but he soon realized he was getting nowhere. His anger vented itself as he stormed out the door, slamming it behind him. After he left, Anna's mother calmed down. She realized she had said too much. Little did she realize what was to come.

Two days later, SS troopers showed up at the door. "You are to come with me," one of them told her mother. "You and the children." He then had a private conversation with Mama.

The whole family was loaded in the back of an old truck. The children had no idea of where they were going or if they would ever see home again. Mama knew, after her private conversation, but she didn't want to frighten the children any more. For two hours, they rode in the truck. They stopped along the way where the troopers showed the children and Mama, trucks

5

loaded with dead bodies, with arms and legs hanging through the rails on the sides of the trucks. Jewish men, women and children, murdered only because of their race.

Their mother protested, pleading and begging the men not to make the children look any longer at these atrocities. As she put out her arm trying to stop them from forcing the children to continue to look, one of the men yanked her arm away, and forced the children to look again.

"I cannot tell you in words, how we felt seeing all those dead bodies," Anna said. "We were shaking and sobbing when we finally drove on." But they weren't through.

They soon arrived at a gateway with a sign, which read, "Dachau Concentration Camp."

"Oh, my God," Anna's mother exclaimed. She tried to pull all seven of the children to her. "Just be real quiet," she said. "Don't cry. God is with us. We have to be brave."

Now, under armed militia, guns pointed at them, they got out of the truck and forced to walk into the camp. One officer became the guide. He took them to the huge ovens, each of these ovens like a huge room in itself. The officer told them that people were tied to stretchers and put into those ovens alive. Others, he said were beaten with their hands and feet tied. Everywhere they looked men, women and children, gaunt with hunger, stood against walls, knowing they were to be shot to death.

Anna said, "My mother didn't say a word, and neither did we. I remember my heart beating in my throat. The fear was burning like fire, but for some reason we couldn't even cry. Somehow, I knew that God wanted us to be brave."

"Let this be a warning to you," the soldier told Anna's mother, in a gentle voice, as he led them back toward the gate. For some reason, he became more considerate. Anna truly believes God changed the officer's heart at that point. He promised her mother he would find out for her where her husband was, and he kept his promise. That was when the army notified them, a few days later, that the Russians held Mr. Rottenfusser as a prisoner of war in Siberia. Anna said, "Mother cried a lot, but at least she had a vague idea of where Papa was and we could only hope that he was alive. Thanks to that wonderful officer who was so kind to us in spite of all the brutality that was going on."

Mama was very upset when the family returned home. She felt responsible for the children having to go through such an ordeal. That trip to Dachau traumatized all the children.

Anna said, "I couldn't sleep at all that night. All I could think of was the truckloads of dead bodies. How could anyone be that cruel and kill all those innocent people. They couldn't help that they were Jewish, just as we couldn't help that we were German."

That night was the beginning of a long series of nightmares for Anna. For years, she would visualize in her dreams, the big ovens where they incinerated live humans. Then she would see herself as sharpshooters shot her while she stood against a brick wall. Then again, she would dream of dead children's arms and legs hanging through the rails of the big trucks. She said, "The nightmares were terrifying."

A few weeks later, as the family sat in their dark apartment, with nothing to do except wait and listen, the air raid siren sounded. Every time this happened, it scared the children. They had seen the tremendous damage that bombs could inflict. They knew of people who had lost their lives in these raids. This particular evening was like many others. When the siren sounded, and with little or no light, they all scrambled to grab whatever they would need or want at the bomb shelter. Stumbling over each other, scared to death they frantically headed out the door. This time the warning almost came too late.

As they ran down the street, they could hear the airplanes approaching. It was a mile from their apartment to the shelter. The roar of the big bombers came closer and closer as they ran as fast as their small legs would carry them. Two men stood at the door to the shelter. They pushed Mama and the children inside and started to shut the doors. Suddenly Mama stopped. She turned and ran back outside. "Mama," they shouted. "Where are you going?" But, she was already out the door.

Fortunately, Mrs. Keller, who always seemed willing to give a helping hand with the children, took them under her wing. They were all crying. They wanted their mother. They were afraid for her safety. They didn't know where she had gone.

Meanwhile, Mama was running frantically back to their apartment. Fearing that at any moment a bomb would drop, she hastened into the building. Taking the steps two and three at a time, she arrived at the door, breathlessly, thankful she had made it that far. She burst through the door and into the children's room, where she found Tilly (Mathilde) sound asleep in her crib. In the rush to get the children safely to the shelter, she had forgotten the baby.

Now, she had to get the baby and herself safely back to the shelter. Wrapping a blanket around the baby, she hit every other step on the way downstairs. Of all the nights to have it happen, this was one of the worst raids they had suffered. As she ran through the streets, planes skimmed the treetops above her head. Explosion after explosion racked the neighborhood. Dirt and smoke filled the air, obscuring her sight. Then a bomb hit close behind her. She threw herself on the ground with Tilly beneath her, trying her best to protect the baby.

Afterward, Mama could not recall how long she lay on the ground with the baby beneath her. She said it must have been hours. Evidently, the concussion rendered her unconscious. When she came to she remembered the baby. Her first thought was that she had suffocated Tilly. Slowly, she lifted herself and rolled away from the baby. Pressing her ear to the baby's chest she listened for a heartbeat. The whole episode hadn't bothered Tilly. She was fast asleep, lying on the ground.

"Thank God," Mama said as she got to her feet, cuddling the baby close. Then, she remembered the other six children. She knew they were safe in the shelter, but they had no way of knowing where Mama was, or if she was safe.

Exhausted and weak from her run through the streets, she stood in the street and looked around. What a catastrophe. Everything within sight was burning to the ground. As she turned to look toward the home where their apartment was she saw that the building was split in two. The houses around it were on fire. But she and Tilly had survived. She gathered herself together, willing herself to walk. She soon met two steel helmeted soldiers on patrol.

"What in the world are you doing and where are you going?" they asked. "You shouldn't be out here with that baby."

As she explained how she had forgotten the baby in the rush to get the family to shelter, they just shook their heads. "You are very lucky to be alive," they told her as they walked with her to the shelter to join the rest of the family.

Back at the shelter, Anna said the six other children waited anxiously, concerned for their mother, not knowing where she was and whether or not she had survived the attack. Six pair of eyes watched the big iron door at the front of the shelter. The tears had dissipated, but the fear for Mama's safety had not.

After a very long and nervous wait, they saw the guard push the door open and Mama walked in carrying Tilly. Then, it all made sense. They had all forgotten about Tilly in their mad dash for shelter. Now Mama and Tilly were safe, and not a moment too soon.

As the guards hastened to shut the door, a bomb exploded right outside. Anna and her siblings were shocked to see one of the guards, his hands still pushing the door closed, literally burn up right before their eyes. Some of the occupants of the shelter screamed, others fell to the ground in fear, but Anna said she and her brothers and sisters just, "stood in a state of shock, watching the horrible scene. The man was solid black from head to toe. Then, another man grabbed a blanket, wrapped the body up and took it away."

The raid continued with one explosion after another. After what they had just experienced, Anna and the others were extremely frightened. For two days, bombs rained down on Munich. The Rottenfusser family and others in the shelter could do nothing but wait. Finally, on the third day, quiet came. Authorities sounded the all clear, and they could return to what was left of their apartment. As mentioned earlier, a large split divided the house in two. There were big holes in the walls. Concussions blew out all the windows. Anna and the others clambered around the ruins, not realizing how dangerous it was.

Anna said, "It looked like the rest of the house would collapse at any moment. We knew it was impossible for us to live there, but there was no place to go. For a few days we slept between broken bricks and piles of dirt and debris. During the daytime, we would climb around the ruins trying to dig out some of our belongings. Mama was constantly in tears." Fortunately, there were some farms not too far away. At night the children would sneak out into the farmer's fields and steal potatoes. Wiping the dirt off as best they could, they ate the potatoes, skin and all. It was their only source of food. They had no way of knowing that this would prepare them for what lay ahead.

Chapter Three

Anna doesn't know how long her mother and the family would have stayed, trying to exist in the bombed out apartment. The government decided this for them just a few days later. Munich had become a very dangerous place to be. Bombing raids became more frequent and more severe. Orders were given that everyone needed to evacuate the city immediately. With nothing but the clothes on their backs, Johanna led the children out into the countryside. They joined a vast parade of people leaving the city with no particular destination in mind.

The only place they knew they weren't going was to another city. The Allied bombers were hitting all the German cities hard. As families and individuals got farther out from the city, they wandered in many directions, knowing it would be hard to find shelter if everyone went the same way. Mama Johanna had a real problem with seven children in tow. Not many people would welcome a family that size. They walked and walked. Three days and three nights they walked. They slept on the side of the road. Whenever they asked for shelter, the answer was always the same. "It is just too much for us to take in eight people."

Then God stepped in and Anna witnessed her first example of someone caring. Footsore, weary and disheartened, the family plodded on. Late on the third day, they approached Mr. Kerster, "a farmer" Anna said, "with a big heart."

"We don't have room for you in the house, but you can stay in the barn," he told them. There was no furniture, no heat, but there was hay and as Anna put it, "At that point we were so tired of walking and the hay was comfortable and fairly warm." Everyone soon fell asleep for their first good rest in three days."

With a rooster for an alarm clock, the family was up early. For the first time in months, they slept without fear. "What a beautiful day it was," Anna said. "We didn't miss the city. Country living was a delight for us kids, even without any conveniences."

God had led them to a family that would do their best to care for Johanna and her children. Once a day, Mr. or Mrs. Kerster would bring food to the barn. It wasn't fancy and there was never any meat. Usually it was a large pot of beans or soup. The only food the Kersters had was what they grew, so sharing meant a great sacrifice on their part. The two families became good friends, sharing what they had and getting to know the other family. Mr. Kerster also got some benefit from this relationship, as Anna and her siblings helped with the chores and in the fields as best they could. It was a new experience for these city bred children and Anna said, "We thoroughly enjoyed the work and had lots of fun."

The children had already learned to go out at night and forage for food, and now this became an every night event. Visiting farms in the area after dark, they were able to find a few vegetables and some fruit to supplement the beans and soup.

Several months went by before the Red Cross finally lent the family a helping hand. The Red Cross was active during the war. They would travel the streets and roads, talking with those who wandered aimlessly, or slept along the road. Somehow, they found out about the Rottenfussers and took pity on them. A small apartment, one bedroom, a kitchen and a bath, became available in the nearby town of Dorfen. There was still no furniture, but they did get some blankets and clothing, and they had a bathroom, an improvement over living in a barn. The government also provided a small amount of food. It wasn't much, one loaf a bread per week for eight people.

Anna said her mother rationed out the food, giving each child a half a slice of bread for breakfast, along with a bowl of what they called coffee. This was hot water with a dark cube of something crumbled into it. Their other ration was white beans. Mama would cook a big pot of beans, which they warmed up each day, eating a little and leaving the rest for the next day. That was the extent of their diet. They were never full or satisfied. They had barely enough to keep their strength. Because it was hard to go to sleep on an empty stomach, there were many times when the children would save their half slice of bread from breakfast, hide it until bedtime and then partake. "A piece of bread never tasted any better than at that moment," Anna told me.

Johanna's parents, Anna's grandparents, Johann and Therese Koenig, lived 215 kilometers or about 36 miles away in the town of Moosach. Anna and the others had experienced very little contact with their grandparents. Their father's mother was deceased and Anna only ever saw her grandfather on her dad's side of the family one time. He had no other contact with the family.

Now a surprise was in order. One day Grandpa Koenig showed up on his bicycle. At age 78, he had quite a bicycle ride. The kids were excited and surprised to see him. The few contacts they had experienced with their grandparents were exciting times for all of them. However, this time, Grandpa brought bad news. As he got off his bike, he was crying and over and over again he moaned the word, "Thea . . .Thea."

Mama Johanna finally understood what he was trying to say. Anna's aunt, her mother Johanna's younger sister, and Grandpa's favorite daughter, had been killed. A bomb struck her house while she was in the kitchen, killing everyone in the house.

This was just one of many tragedies to strike the Rottenfusser family in those days. A few weeks later, a telegram arrived for Mama telling her that Anna's uncle, Johanna's brother, had been killed on the Russian front. Two more aunts and uncles and their families on the Rottenfusser side of the family also died as the result of the war. It was a sad time, a shock for Mama, as tragedy after tragedy seemed to strike the family. They shed tears, but life had to go on.

After Grandpa returned home, and with one tragedy after another striking the family, Anna's mother became very nervous, worrying about her parents. She paced the floor day and night, barely getting any sleep. She had acquired a used bicycle and the Kersters had given the family a small wagon. Mama hitched the wagon to the bike, put the smaller children in the wagon, and while the other children walked, she pedaled the bike pulling the small ones, headed for her parent's home.

Anna commented, "Today, something like that would look strange, but in those days it was our only transportation. A bicycle to us at that time was like having a Cadillac today."

To get to the town of Moosach, the family had to go around the edge of Munich for some distance. "The closer we got to Munich, the more destruction we saw," Anna said. "Miles and miles away it seemed like everything was on fire. Munich was in flames. Because of the devastation and fires, the family had to take a long detour before arriving in Moosach. Munich had been bombed to the ground."

The children were in awe. They had no words to describe it. Anna said their eyes got bigger and bigger.

Then, as they walked alongside Mama pedaling the bike, they saw an unbelievable sight. On the horizon, stood one building, completely unscathed from the bombing. Their home church, St. George Catholic Church stood proud, its steeple tall above the wreckage all around. Anna said, "It looked like God standing there as tall as He could be, saying, 'Come all my children, I will watch over you."

Here we see God and one of his miracles. He was at work, even in the midst of devastation.

Mama Johanna decided they should head to the church and pray before they continued on to her parent's home. It would give them a chance to rest as well as pray. Pedaling and walking, some time later, they found themselves at St. George. They were surprised to find, when they walked in, that the church was full of people. Several months before, the authorities ordered everyone to leave Munich, but it was obvious that some had come to the church for shelter. Little groups of people occupied much of the space. Wounded people were lying on the pews. Little children, frightened and hungry cried for attention.

Mama and the children wandered through the crowd, looking for a place to rest and to pray. As they moved by one corner, Mama did a double take. She looked at the people huddled there, looked away and then quickly looked back. "Mama! Papa!" She ran toward the group and then Anna and her siblings also spotted Grandpa and Grandma. Anna said they were "huddled up like a pair of pigeons. We could see in their eyes how happy they were to see us." God was at work bringing this family back together for a little while.

Anna said her grandfather seldom cried, but now he and his wife both had tears in their eyes as they hugged their daughter and the children. Grandpa had fought in WW I and witnessed the devastation then. Now he was experiencing it for a second time and in the process had lost four of his children. "Even for a man, it was too much to handle," Anna commented.

Others nearby made room for the family and they settled in to spend the night. The next day they all went to check on Grandpa and Grandma's house. Evidently, the bombings and the fires had quieted down, as several others left that morning to check on their homes

Everyone was pleasantly surprised to find the house in good shape. The grandparents had a few days to reacquaint themselves with their daughter and her family. The time came when they needed to get back home, so the wagon was loaded with the smaller children and the trek toward home, pedaling and walking began.

They arrived back home without incident and settled in, but it wouldn't be long before another disruption would occur. Once again, they listened day and night to their radio, but there were no air raids or alarms. It seemed like things had quieted down. Then, on a quiet Sunday afternoon, one of the neighbors came running through the neighborhood shouting, "The Americans are coming. American soldiers are coming." The invasion of Germany by the Allies was well under way.

Not knowing what to expect, and having heard all kinds of rumors, everyone ran to their homes, locking windows and doors. It wasn't long until American tanks came rolling down the street, followed by troops of soldiers. To the Germans, this was the enemy. Anna said, "This was a terrifying moment for all of us. Mother was a very strong woman, but even she was afraid."

Three nights later they had reason to be afraid. There was a loud knock at the door. It was nighttime and everyone was in bed. Mrs. Rottenfusser opened the door to find three American soldiers, armed with machine guns. One of them brushed past her and looked around. The children heard the noise and were now huddled together in a corner of the room. Then, the two soldiers at the door ordered all of them out. "Raus! Raus!" (Out! Out!) they demanded. Now the children were crying. Their mother was trying to find clothes to dress them and wanting to pack a few things, but the soldiers ordered them to leave immediately. Still in their nightclothes, and with no time to pack anything, the family left, not knowing where they would find a place to sleep.

This was a harsh reality of war. The soldiers had orders to find a temporary headquarters for the invading army and they were following orders.

As they left their home, Mama said, "Maybe we should go back to the Kersters." Excitedly, one of the kids said, "Yeah. Maybe we can sleep in the barn again." They were soon on their way. The Kersters welcomed them and they settled down once more in the barn. They found out that the Kersters were supplying the U.S. troops with vegetables from the farm. Because of this, the United Sates Army allowed the Kersters to stay in their home. Unfortunately, this meant there were no vegetables for the Rottenfussers. They did have a roof over their heads, but that didn't keep them from starving.

With the invasion troops taking up all the crops that were grown, the kids had no choice but to sneak back into town each night and scavenge in the garbage pails. The U.S. Army had taken over the entire town. So Anna and her siblings would go late at night and go through their garbage cans, finding stale bread, powdered milk, sugar cubes, and occasionally canned food that had not been opened. Not able to read English, they had no idea what these ration tins held, but they took them back to the barn, pried them open and ate.

At four a.m., the children would walk to the landfill where the occupation army dumped their garbage. The soldiers soon recognized them and some took pity. They started setting aside things they felt the family could use. One day they gave the kids a closed five-gallon bucket full of dried vegetables. When they brought it home, their mother was suspicious. She felt it might be a bomb. She was afraid to open it, but finally decided, "If it is, so be it." They were pleased when it did not explode and more pleased when they saw the vegetables.

"With the food the Americans had thrown away we were able to stay alive," Anna said, "and it always tasted good. Mother had always said what a sin it was to throw away good food, but this time, even she was glad when we found some."

They existed this way for several months. Always afraid someone would catch them, they were very careful as they sneaked around the backs of the houses in town looking for scraps in the garbage that were edible. They were still able to get their one loaf of bread each week, which meant a half slice apiece each morning, but food became more and more scarce and hunger a continuing problem. Water was also a problem. Always thirsty, their throats dry and parched, officials told them not to drink the water because of the fear of typhoid fever. Young and not understanding about disease, they started drinking from toilets whenever the opportunity presented itself. This was the only water they could find, and mama did not know what they were doing.

Before long, Anna became ill. She could not walk. She had a high fever. Her chest was swollen and hurt. Her arms and legs became swollen and twisted. She said, her "elbows were in front and her knees in back. I was unable to get up on my feet." Her siblings were soon as bad as Anna. Their bodies ached and were swollen and deformed. They had no muscle control. Mama left to find a doctor. He soon confirmed her worst fear. The children all had typhoid fever. His prognosis was not good. He said their chance of survival was slim. The typhoid fever had ravaged their bodies already weakened from malnutrition. "All you can do," the doctor told Mama, "is wait and see. There is nothing more that I can do. There is no medicine available. There is a war going on." With that, he left Mama Johanna with her seven children, who were all desperately ill.

Their mother became a twenty-four hour nurse, moving from one child to the next, trying somehow to bring their temperatures down. No one else came near. Typhoid was very communicable. It had become an epidemic in that area. Lying in the hay in a barn, not even a bed to rest in, it was a wonder, a miracle that the children were still alive. Their mother would not give up. That was one time in her life when Anna's mother prayed fervently.

Ten days went by with no change. The doctor's word had discouraged their Mother to the point she was afraid she would lose all of her children. On the tenth day, the doctor returned. This time he had an American Army doctor with him. Again, God provided. The American doctor checked each of the children, shook his head solemnly and then quickly left.

Then, thirty minutes later, he reappeared. He had gone to get medicine, which he gave to Mama. She was very hesitant to take anything from an American. Anna said, "He gently put his hand on Mother's shoulder. 'It's okay,' he told her."

The two doctors had a short discussion and then instructed Johanna to start the medicine immediately. She continued her twenty-four hour a day vigil. Once again, God answered prayers. Three days later, the fever finally broke. It just so happened that the German doctor came by that day to check on his patients. Surprised and pleased, he couldn't believe how effective the medicine worked. Checking each of the seven children, he looked at their mother and said, "Mother, it's time for you to get some rest. The danger is over. The kids are going to make it."

The typhoid along with malnutrition had taken its toll. The children were still very week. Elbows and knees were still deformed, but the fever was gone and the typhoid was under control.

The doctor had additional good news for Mrs. Rottenfusser. He told her the U.S. Army doctor had taken a great interest in the family. He was concerned for their welfare. He had even arranged for the family to move back into their apartment. As the children regained their strength and were able to move, they found their apartment ready and waiting. Their mother had cried for weeks over her seven children, and now her tears were tears of happiness because they were back in their home.

It wasn't long before the family would experience another scare.

Chapter Four

Let us review for a moment. The Nazis forced Anna and her siblings, as small children, to walk through a concentration camp and see trucks loaded with dead bodies, people waiting to be killed by firing squads, and huge ovens where people were burned alive. Their lives had already suffered great trauma. Then the family moved from their home when bombs destroyed it, and again when foreign troops took over their country. They lived in a barn and had to scavenge for food in garbage cans and drink water from a toilet. The result is that typhoid fever struck down all seven children, and as they started to feel better, they thought; *At last things seem to be getting back toward normal.* However, they were wrong.

Anna and her siblings settled down once again in the small apartment. There still was not nearly enough food, and the children continued to feel the ravages of typhoid and malnutrition. But, they were home.

Then, a few short weeks later, a big grey bus pulled up out in front. It was a Red Cross bus. Several Red Cross nurses swept into the house, picking up all seven children and carrying them to the bus. Momma started crying, quickly followed by the children's wails.

What is happening? Where are they taking us? Why won't they let our mother come with us?

One of the nurses explained to their mother and then she told them, as all of them wept, that there is great concern that the combination of typhoid and malnutrition would cripple them for the rest of their lives. "If you want to walk again, you must go," mother told the children. "I will come and pick you up and bring you home when the doctor says it is okay."

They finally calmed down, but they were still not sure what was going to happen to them, or if they would ever see their home and their mother again.

Anna said that the place the Red Cross took them was very beautiful. Called Schleedorf, it was. originally built as a convent. They turned it into a hospital because of the war. Sitting on a hilltop, away from the city, it was reasonably safe. Best of all, for the first time in a long time they had beds to sleep in, rather than hay on the floor. There were fifty-eight beds in one room, but the children did not complain. The nurses were nuns who gave them very good care, the food was good as well as plentiful, and everyone treated them well. Slowly, but surely their strength in their arms and legs returned, with the good food, medication and lots of therapy. Eventually all of them were able to walk again and felt much better.

Their mother had a year to herself. It took that long for their bodies to heal. One morning Sister Andrea came to their seven beds carrying a armload of new clothes. "It's time to get dressed," she told them. "I have a surprise for you."

Not knowing what the surprise was, they got dressed. She led down the long hallway, and through a wide glass door that led to a beautiful garden area. Anna's sister Johanna was the first to spot their mother Johanna. "Mother," she screamed. All seven children rushed to greet their mother, the first time they had seen her in a year. She greeted them warmly, all but Anna.

I asked Anna why her mother had not come to visit and she said the hospital did not allow visitors for fear she would bring germs into the hospital or that she would carry germs out to her neighbors and friends. So for a solid year the children never saw their mother and she did not see them. Even then, Anna realized that her mother did not have the same love for her that she had for the other children. Anna says that until this day, she still sheds tears when she thinks about their relationship. She has no idea why her mother favored the others, but didn't love her. A little later we will see affirmation of this. It wasn't just in Anna's imagination.

The war neared its end, but the bombers still flew their sorties. Once again, God spared Anna and her siblings. Just a few days after they left Schleedorf, a bomb struck the hospital, destroying the hospital and killing everyone inside.

Chapter Five

Those of you who know your history, know that in June 1945 the war in Europe ended. The war in the Pacific would end a couple months later, after two atom bombs destroyed Nagasaki and Hiroshima Japan.

The battle for survival in Germany would continue for some time. German cities, like Munich and Essen had to be completely rebuilt. Unexploded bombs, particularly phosphate bombs were numerous. Cleanup became a priority everywhere. People searched through the rubble for their belongings or things they could use in rebuilding and getting on with their lives. Searching through rubble to find possessions, some lost their lives as they stepped on these bombs, or accidentally hit them with tools.

Slowly, they rebuilt their cities. Things gradually started to return to normal. However, the scars, the broken hearts for lost loved ones, or destroyed homes, would cause nightmares and loneliness for years to come. Anna said this seemed to affect children the most. She added, "Especially for me."

Germany was plunged into a depression. There was nothing to buy. Money was almost worthless. The government rationed food using stamps, which provided some food, but in limited amounts. It wasn't starvation, neither was it "all you can eat."

Anna yearned to hear from her father. The last they knew, he was in Siberia Russia, but they had not heard from him and did not know if he was still alive. They looked for a letter from him, but it never came. They saw other men, fathers and brothers, neighbors who came home from the war, but their father was not one of them.

The aftermath of the war, all that they had gone through, and now the fact that they knew nothing of their father's fate, began to work on Anna's mother. Anna said, "We began to see a big change in her. One day she met a woman who then started coming by the house each day. She was a fortune-teller. She taught Mother how to lay out and read cards. Mother would sit each evening, long after we went to bed, laying out cards. Friends started coming by, and it seemed like the whole town knew about Mother and how she read cards. There were people in our house every day. She even had people who came by to thank her, because what she had told them had come true."

Anna said that at night, when she went to bed, she would beg God to bring her dad home from wherever he was.

She was also worried about her mother and the change that had come over her. She became very bitter. The sad part was that Momma took out her bitterness on Anna. Her mother continually criticized her. One day, Anna took a small sip of milk without asking. She knew she shouldn't do it, but she did not expect the beating her mother gave her. This was not a spanking. Blood came out of her ears, nose and mouth, as well as bleeding cuts on her back from the belt her mother used to beat her. This was not an isolated incident. It seemed that Anna could not please her mother. Quite often she was beaten with the leather belt.

Anna said her older sister Johanna intervened or their mother would probably have killed Anna. "She had no control of herself," Anna said. "We were never allowed to take anything to eat or drink without asking first."

Food was still scarce. The children still got hungry. Anna said she was always hungry and it was not easy as a child, to resist the temptation to take something to eat. Her mother constantly using Anna as the scapegoat exacerbated the problem. Anna said that her sisters would take things without asking, and their mother would not punish them. However, her mother would even punish Anna when someone else had helped themselves, and they would blame Anna. She even resorted to telling her mother who the culprit was, but her siblings would deny the blame, and Anna once more got the belt.

It is not unusual for a child to feel that they are the one being picked on, or singled out for punishment, but as we will see a little later, Anna had good reason to remember these events correctly. It got so bad that she would lock herself in the bathroom and "cry my heart out."

Anna was now in the second grade and one afternoon her teacher, Mrs. Beck, asked her to stay after school. "She said she wanted to talk to me. I was scared to death. *What did I do now?* I asked myself. I was always very quiet in school. I never spoke or raised my hand. I was very shy. In fact, I had such a fear complex that I would often stutter when I was asked to say something. This caused everyone in the family to make fun of me."

Anna said even at the table, when her siblings asked for more food, when it was available, she would stammer, not able to say "please". The others would laugh and that would make her cry. Then her mother would get angry with her and Anna would leave the table hungry. Even to recite at school would leave her in tears. *"Maybe that is why Mrs. Beck wants to talk to me,"* she thought.

Mrs. Beck had seen the swollen eyes and she asked Anna what was wrong. She put her arms around Anna and told her that she could be trusted. This brought more tears. "I want to help you," She said, "but I can't help if you won't tell me what is wrong."

It was a strange feeling for Anna, to find someone who seemed to care very much. Her mother had never told her she loved her. She had never held Anna in her arms or kissed her. As we talked in my study one day, I asked Anna why her mother treated her the way she did. Anna's eyes filled with tears as she said, "I don't know. I have tried all of my life to understand and I still don't."

As she talked with her teacher that day many years ago, she finally realized she could tell Mrs. Beck the truth. "Last night," she said, "I overheard my mother talking with another lady. They were talking about me. Mother said, 'I just don't feel anything for her and I don't love her. She would be better off with you before I lose control with her one of these days. I'll get her things together and you can pick her up next week.'" Then Anna added, "I sneaked back to bed and cried all night."

Then she told Mrs. Beck that she did not want to leave her home. "I love my sisters and brothers and I love my mother. I would rather take the beatings than to have to leave home."

Mrs. Beck was a good listener. As Anna poured out her troubles, with tears in her eyes and her head in her teacher's lap, Mrs. Beck held her tight and promised to talk to her mother. Anna asked her not to go to her mother, but she said, "It is my duty to talk with her and see if I can help." And she did.

The results were about as Anna expected. She got in trouble for talking with her teacher and ended up with her mother using the belt on her once more. She not only received the worst beating that she had suffered, her mother gave her nothing to eat for three days. Knowing hunger almost all of her life had not prepared Anna for what she called "the worst punishment of all." Her sister Johanna was her only friend for those three days. She saved her bread from their morning ration and gave it to Anna. Then, one evening they had pancakes and Johanna was able to sneak one away from the table for her sister. Hiding it under her blouse, so their mother would not see it, she said she had to go to the bathroom, but instead took the pancake to Anna in their room.

Johanna knew of her mother's plan to give Anna to this other lady. She assured Anna that she would come to see her. This gave Anna a small amount of hope for the future, which looked very bleak for a second grader.

A few days later, Anna's new parents came to get her. "It was a sad moment for me," Anna said. "The people were very nice, but I didn't care about anything except staying home where I thought I belonged. I pleaded with my mother and I begged her to please let me stay. I tried to put my arms around her but she didn't want any part of me, so I left with my new parents. They tried very hard to calm me down, but I couldn't stop crying. My eyes were all puffy, my nose was running, and my heart was broken."

I asked Anna the names of her new parents and she said she honestly could not remember. The pictures of them and all of Anna's early childhood were destroyed She did say that they were very kind to her. For the first time in her life, she had her own bedroom and her own bed. At home there had been four girls in one room and two to a bed. They bought her clothes and they showed love to her. She felt spoiled. She said, "To them, I was their little princess." They had no children of their own and were unable to have children. As the months went by Anna learned to love them. She said there wasn't anything they would not do for her. "I began to feel what happiness was, for the very first time."

One day, her stepfather came home with a beautiful, brand new flute. Anna's stepmother was a music teacher and she gave Anna lessons. Anna said, I remember the beautiful songs I learned. Playing the flute was a real joy to me. I loved music and I learned fast."

Things went very well for Anna for a year. She was thrilled as that year neared completion and her new parents asked her if she would like to live with them forever. They had decided to adopt her and make her a permanent part of their family as their only child. Anna was thrilled. She had learned to love them and she knew they loved her. She still thought about her siblings and her father. She wondered if she would ever see her father again. She even thought about her mother. The hurt was gone. She was happy, but she still had love for her family.

The adoption papers were drawn up. The only thing needed to finalize the adoption was her mother's signature. The afternoon came when they were to meet and her mother would sign the papers. Her stepparents waited anxiously and Anna said she felt nervous. She was afraid and didn't like the idea that her mother was coming.

Her premonition was correct. When her mother rang the bell at the front door of her stepparents, Anna went to her bedroom to wait. In just a few moments the door burst open and her mother came into her bedroom saying, "You're coming home with me." Anna stood in a state of shock. Her mother ordered her, "Pack your things. You are coming home."

Anna started to cry and that didn't help the situation. A big argument ensued between Anna, her stepparents and her mother. The end result was that Anna left with her mother, who fussed at her and jerked her arm because Anna couldn't stop crying.

"I was glad to see my oldest sister, Johanna again, and she was glad to see me," Anna told me. "But the rest were as bitter as my mother was. My Cinderella dream had come to an end."

For weeks she would lie in her bed at night thinking of her foster parents and the beautiful things they had provided her with. Once again she turned to God, asking him why she had to give all of that up. Her Catholic upbringing had taught her a little about God, but it sounded as though He was unreachable way off up in heaven somewhere. Yet, somehow, she knew to pray to Him and she hoped that He heard her prayers.

Almost two years later a neighbor told her that both of her foster parents had passed away. That they had grieved over losing their only daughter. Her mother forbid her to even mention their names, but it took several years for her to get over their deaths.

Chapter Six

The next few years were not easy ones for Anna. Her mother treated her like a servant girl. By age ten, she felt like an adult. Her mother did not allow her to have friends, to play with other children or to even talk with others outside of school. Her only chance to communicate with children her own age was going to and from school. It was a long walk, and she knew as she approached home, to separate herself from the other children she walked with.

"I was always scared to death that my mother would see me walking with someone other than my sisters. Whenever that happened, and it did happen occasionally, I got the belt."

Just before Christmas, a classmate asked Anna to walk home with her. She said her mother had a gift for Anna. Not having received many gifts in her life, Anna was very excited, anxious for school to finish for the day. Many families with children in the school knew that the Rottenfusser family was poor. With no father at home and mother not working, that was quite obvious. Anna said that the pastor came by the house once a week and brought a little food and clothing to help. So, Anna was not surprised that one of the mothers of a classmate had a little gift for her at Christmastime.

As soon as school was out, the two girls hurried to Elfriede's house. Anna was overwhelmed that her parents had put together a beautiful fruit basket. After graciously thanking the family, Anna started home. As she walked along she also started worrying. Her mother had forbid her to bring any kind of gift home with her. Such a beautiful basket of fruit was too tempting. In fact, Anna would have eaten some of the fruit before she got home, but the fear that her mother would smell it on her breath, or some other way know she had eaten from the basket, kept her from doing so.

She said, as she climbed the stairs to their second floor apartment and reached the door, "My heart started to beat faster. With my hands full, I couldn't open the door so I rang the doorbell. My sister opened the door and as soon as I saw her face I knew I was in trouble. As I walked in the door I was knocked from one side of the room to the other. Fruit rolled in every direction. Some of it went under the couch, some under the table. It was all over the floor. Mother was waiting behind the door and she let me know she was angry because I was late getting home. She knew to the minute how long it took to walk home. Mother had strong hands and she knew how to hurt you. I tried to explain why I was late, but she didn't want to listen. I ended up getting beaten with the leather belt.

"To make matters worse I had to go to school the next morning with face all swollen and my eyes red from crying. When class was over Elfriede asked me what was wrong. I told her and somehow that drew the two of us close together. We became best friends. She seemed to feel that it was partly her fault. I explained that it was not, it was mine. I should have known better. For some reason I was the black sheep in our family, and it hurt."

Neighbors soon realized that Anna's relationship with her mother was not good. They saw Anna go to school quite often with tear stained eyes. They would smile at Anna, and quite often someone would give her an apple or a candy bar once she was out of sight of home. With it came the warning to not let her mother know.

As mentioned earlier, this puzzles Anna to this day. She has never understood why her mother did not love her. She always did her share around the house. With seven children, there was always a lot to do. Her mother never allowed Anna to go to bed early. She worked late every night doing an unending list of chores. When she was ill, she didn't dare tell anyone. If she told her sisters, they would tell their mother, and then Anna was in trouble.

Once every two weeks, was washday. The washroom was in the basement and used by all of the families living there. Therefore, it was necessary to do your wash on the assigned days. Yes, days. It took three days every two weeks to do the Rottenfusser family wash. This was no Laundromat. There were no washing machines or dryers. Mama Johanna started by taking all the white clothes and boiling them in a large kettle. Then, one by one, they scrubbed each item on a big table with a brush, piece by piece.

Then the rinsing process began. They rinsed everything three times. When Anna returned from school, she joined her mother in the process standing on her feet until midnight, when her mother would finally tell her to go to bed.

"I was used to hard work and late hours," Anna said. "That was expected. However, there was never a time in my life when my mother rewarded me for doing anything. She wasn't the type to tell anyone, 'You did a good job,' or 'I appreciated what you did.' And, she never showed any affection toward me at all. I tried so very hard to do things right, but the harder I tried, the more I got into trouble."

Anna said that over time she became very bitter toward herself. She would look at her sisters and see how happy they seemed to be. At Christmas, or on other special occasions, their presents were always much more expensive than Anna's. This was not just her imagination. She would never forget her mother giving her away to another couple, and then just as Anna got used to being treated nicely, she was carried back home. There was a great difference between the way she was treated, in comparison to her sisters. She remembered one Christmas very vividly. Like all children, Christmas was a special time. On this particular day, one of her sisters got a beautiful new coat. Another got a dress and sweater. All of the other children got beautiful gifts. Anna received an inexpensive scarf and pair of gloves. Anna said, "I kept looking for another present. I thought Santa had forgotten something. But I was wrong. We always had our celebration at midnight on Christmas Eve. After we opened our present, we had punch and cookies, and other goodies Mother had baked. I guess I showed my disappointment that I had not gotten gifts comparable to my sisters. Mother sent me to bed without any treats. I wanted to run away, to anywhere, just far away. The feeling I had, carried over to New Year's Eve. I was still so upset and bitter, I did not wish anyone a Happy New Year. This upset my mother even more and once again I went to bed without any treats."

The next spring, when Anna was ten, the Rottenfussers had a pleasant surprise. On May 9, 1949, late at night, the doorbell rang. As the family awoke, everyone questioned who would be at the door at that time of a night. Mother Johanna went to the door and as she opened it, she screamed. Somehow, everyone sensed this was a happy scream and all seven kids headed for the door.

At first glance, it appeared to be a skinny man dressed in raggedy clothes. But a second look excited them all. It was Daddy, home at last after spending seven years, four of those years after the war was over, as a prisoner of war at a camp in Siberia. Most of the rest of the night the family sat and listened as he told story after story about Russia and how cruel the Russians were, and how they treated the prisoners. He told how he was forced to watch as the Russians cut out the eyes of his best friend. He was lucky to have survived. He was glad to be home. The children were thrilled to see him for the first time in seven years, and the first time ever for Hans, the youngest, who had born after his daddy had left for the war. Finally, exhaustion ruled and Daddy told everyone it was time to go to bed.

Anna was thrilled. She loved her Dad and she felt that because he was now home, things would be much better. "I told myself, it will be better now," she said, "and before I went to sleep, I thanked God for bringing Daddy home."

Everything seemed to better now that Dad was home. The government hired him and gave him a good job. The family was whole for the first time in a long time. Life seemed normal. Mama Johanna could quit worrying about their father.

However, the good times did not last long. One evening, three months later, Papa Johann didn't come home from work. The family soon discovered he met another woman and had left the family to be with her. Divorce papers were filed and acted on. The seven Rottenfusser children were once again without a father in the home. Their mother was more bitter than ever. Their Dad did come for a few hours every other week, but it wasn't like having a father.

Anna said, "I always loved Dad, no matter what." Perhaps, the saddest part of the divorce was that Dad asked if Anna could come and live with him and her mother said absolutely no.

Anna cried out again to God, the only place she had to go for solace.

But she was growing up and it wouldn't be long before she would find some new interests.

Chapter Seven

Three years passed without any serious incident. Anna and her siblings were moving up through the grades. At age thirteen, Anna finished her last year in school. Age thirteen was graduation age for German children at that time.

Her dream was to be a dressmaker or a secretary. Unfortunately, good jobs were very difficult to come by. Germany was still in the throes of a post-war depression. The government ran everything with an iron hand, and young people didn't get much choice of career opportunities. The government added available workers to a list. When your name came to the top, if you did not take the job offered you, your name went back to the bottom of the list. It would be a long time before you received another offer.

Anna was somewhat reluctant to leave school. She enjoyed school and her teachers. Her favorite teacher taught the seventh grade, her last year in school. Miss Hilde Greissle became one of Anna's friends as well as her teacher. That friendship endured for many years after Anna left school.

Anna wanted to find work. She knew she needed to find a job and yet no one she knew, or was able to contact, was looking for help.

When her sisters completed their schooling, they all went to work in local factories. The family's financial situation was not good, so every income helped out. Her brother Helmut became a carpenter, doing framing and roofing.

Anna was different. Her entire family mocked her. Her mother had often told her, "You don't amount to anything." "You are stupid." "You are ugly." Anna became very shy and withdrawn. She stuttered when she became the least bit upset, and that caused her siblings to make fun of her. They would laugh, which would make her cry, and she withdrew even more. She got to the point where she hated herself. However, it also made her more determined to make something of herself, to get some kind of training or to learn a trade.

Then one afternoon, her aunt whose name she carried, Aunt Anna came by to visit. Her Aunt had a friend who owned a flower shop. She was looking for a girl she could train to become a florist. Her aunt suggested Anna go and talk with her. This did not fit in with Anna's dreams of being a secretary or a dressmaker, but a job was a job. Anna loved flowers, and the more she thought about it, the more attractive it seemed. She decided to give it a try. She went for an interview and Anna said, "This was my first big step in life."

Her schooling had prepared Anna well for this experience. Her teachers taught her how to dress for a job, how to speak, how to act responsibly, and how to accept the duties that came with a new job. So this thirteen year old girl had been trained to act like a mature adult, something other schools and parents need to learn as they take on the responsibility of young teens.

Anna deserves much more credit here than she will admit to. She mentioned that many parents went with their children to job interviews, and did most of the talking. In doing research for another book, I found this to be true even with college graduates in the United States today. But at age thirteen, Anna was prepared and she set forth.

She said, "I was glad I had no one to talk for me. My mother gave me a complex because she always was critical of what I did. I had a tremendous fear of her. I had more confidence when I went alone."

Her teacher had taught her never to be late. Her mother never allowed her to roam around Munich, Anna knew only the way to school and to church. Afraid she might get lost, she left the house very early. As she expected, she did lose her way. She was riding the bus and it passed her stop before she realized it. When she got off at the next stop, she became disoriented. She looked for a bus or streetcar that was going in the wrong direction. Then, she discovered she had lost her wallet. Now she had no choice but to walk. She walked as fast as she could, asking for help all along the way just to be sure she was headed in the right direction.

Finally, she arrived, an hour and a half late. She was very hesitant about going in, her emotions torn, between going in and facing ridicule for being so late for an appointment, or going home and having her mother chastise her. As she thought about what she would tell her mother and her mother's reaction, she decided she would rather face the owner of the flower shop. Once again, she turned to God. "Please help me," she prayed and walked in, frightened to death. She forgot what to say to introduce herself. "I just stood there in my long pigtails," she said, a frightened thirteen-year-old girl

An older woman came from the back and said, "May I help you?"

Anna finally was able to blurt out through her tears, who she was and why she was late. At that point, words left her, and she stood not knowing what to expect.

What she received was kindness and understanding. Miss Wagner, the owner took Anna under her wing. After a guided tour of the large, well-equipped workshop, she asked Anna a few questions, even asking about her siblings.

It was not easy work, she warned Anna. The hours were from seven a.m. until eight p.m. It was a long work week, a full day on Saturday and a half day on Sunday. Finally, she said, "If you would like to work here, the job is yours."

Anna was elated. Without hesitation, she agreed to learn to become a florist. "Yes," she said, "This is exactly what I want to do."

The owner gave Anna bus fare to get back home, shook her hand and Anna was convinced that this kind and generous woman was someone she would enjoy having as an employer.

School finished in September, and on December 1, 1952, Anna started her new job. Long hours and very little pay didn't keep her from enjoying her first work experience. Six marks a week, the equivalent of three dollars is not a lot of money especially for the hours she worked each week, but at the end of the first year the pay increased to eight marks and in the third year to ten marks. Anna's motivation came from the fact that after the three years of training, she would make a lot more money, and she was working for someone who seemed to appreciate her work. The wages were not that important. Her mother took all that she earned, except for the bus fare to go back and forth. She worked hard for long hours each week, but accepted the fact that she had a lot to learn.

Her training was not limited to her work in the shop. One day a week she attended business college from eight a.m. to five p.m. where she learned the botanical names of flowers, grass and trees, the history of these plants and other information vital to her work as a florist. Anna found it interesting, realizing that this was information she needed to know to do her job correctly.

Miss Wagner was a Master Florist, very strict, but always fair. She treated Anna well and Anna said she taught her well.. "If you watch me," Miss Wagner told her, "you can learn a lot from your eyes. If you do what I tell you, you can be just like me."

Anna respected Miss Wagner and her abilities, so she found this to be good advice. She desired to be the best and she felt that she had a good teacher.

The florist shop did a good business and Miss Wagner assigned Anna the delivery duties, which took her all across Munich. She soon became familiar with the city of her birth, but one her mother had not allowed her to explore. She enjoyed being outdoors. Miss Wagner provided the bicycle, and no matter the weather, Anna and the bike were seen all across Munich. There were a few occasions where she had to make deliveries as far as sixty kilometers (36 miles).away. These were daylong trips and Miss Wagner got upset when Anna did not arrive back at the shop just when she should have.

Anna said, "Sometimes when I was out like that I enjoyed the beautiful countryside or the small towns I rode through. My mind would wander and I would dream of what I hoped life would be like someday. I asked her what those dreams were and she replied, "A better life. Someone to love me, beautiful things to own and children. But the most important of all was some one to love."

She said there were times when she would get off the bike and walk, pushing the bike, taking deep breaths of the clean fresh air. She would sing as she walked, happy to have a chance to enjoy life. Then she added, "I never passed a church. No matter where I was, if I saw a church I would stop, go inside and take time for a short prayer. Even when I came near a church I was familiar with, I would go out of my way to go there and pray. I didn't know much about God, but somehow I knew He was with me."

No doubt her daydreaming and taking time to visit nearby churches and pray, explained why Anna was sometimes late in getting back to the flower shop.

God worked in Anna's life in some rather mysterious ways. One day when she left for work, her mother seemed very depressed, Anna was much more conscious of her mother's needs than vice versa, Anna had a two-hour lunch break and she decided to go home and check on her mother. Riding the bike home, she found her mother still depressed. After some questioning, her mother admitted that their financial position worried her, particularly the fact that there was never enough food for the eight of them. As they talked her mother started crying, because she didn't know what she would feed the family that evening. Anna was perplexed. She didn't know what more she could do to help. Then, she got an idea. It was mushroom season. She decided she would take the rest of her lunch hour to go look for mushrooms. They had fed the family more than once after the war. The problem was that many other families knew of the same spot that Anna did where they found mushrooms. It was very late in the day to find anything there. Her mother told her, "You won't find anything. We're not the only ones who live off mushrooms."

Anna persisted and she took off on the bicycle. She loved her mother, but had never received love in return. She yearned to find some way to win her mother's approval, a compliment, just a kind word. She was determined that this day she would find some mushrooms and that when she brought them home that her mother would be appreciative.

When she arrived at the spot, she put down her bike and started walking. Back and forth she looked. Her two-hour lunchtime was up and still she had found nothing, not one mushroom. She was shocked when she looked at her watch and realized it was already three o'clock. She was to have been back at work at two. Discouraged, she sat down on the ground and cried. She wanted so much to do something to please her mother. "*I can not go home empty handed*." she thought. "*Why dear God? Why?*"

She told me, "I always had my private conversations with God. I thought He was so far away and unreachable. Yet, I always talked to Him. He was my secret friend. I would ask, 'God hold me while I cry.' I was so disappointed not finding one single mushroom. I sat down on a big rock where my bike was lying and I cried out to God, "Why?" I was so sure that I would find mushrooms. Now I would have to go home and hear my mother telling me, 'I told you so.' With my face buried in my apron, I cried and cried. Suddenly, I felt someone touching my shoulder. I jumped up frightened and afraid, but I did not see anyone. *I must be dreaming*, I thought to myself. I picked up my bike, ready to go home. Then I saw a tiny mushroom peeking through the wheel of my bike. As I looked down and then around, I couldn't believe my eyes and what I saw. There were mushrooms everywhere. I knew I couldn't have been that blind before. I reached down and touched one. They were real. I was sitting in the middle of a whole field of mushrooms."

Jumping up, Anna went to work. She found a large box nearby. She picked mushrooms until the box was full, laughing and crying at the same time. Even after she had filled the box, there were many mushrooms all around.

"As I pedaled home, my heart was full of joy," she said. "I never realized at the time what a tremendous miracle God had performed."

Her mother exclaimed, "I can tell by the look on your face that you found some. I can't believe it, all these mushrooms."

Expectation of praise from her mother was short-lived. Anna wanted to share her experience with her mother about what had happened. But she said, "Mother didn't hear a word of it. She was so wrapped up in her mushrooms. She cleaned them and cooked a pot full for supper. The rest she traded to neighbors for bread and milk." There would be no words of praise for Anna, or for God.

Before you lay it off to Anna's imagination or poor eyesight, remember that during the 1948 Israel-Arab war, the Jewish women found a spinach-like weed that suddenly sprouted in many fields and provided food at a time when it was much needed.

You might also recall that God provided manna & quail for the Israelites wandering in the desert for 40 years. God does provide when we have the faith to believe.

Anna had missed a whole afternoon at work and the next problem was what to tell Miss Wagner. Her mother wrote a note telling her boss that she had been needed desperately at home. However, Anna felt she had to tell the truth. After she had finished the story of how God had answered her plea, Miss Wagner discounted it by saying she probably had not seen things correctly the first time she looked. The miracle was Anna's. No one else believed. She knew in her heart that she was not that blind. There had been absolutely nothing the first time she walked through the field. Then suddenly she was sitting in the middle of a whole patch. of mushrooms. And, these were not just ordinary mushrooms. The Germans called them Herbal Blatter (huge mushrooms) named Autumn Leaves, the best tasting of all mushrooms. Anna said, "I knew it was God. Only He could perform a miracle like that. It was a miracle I will never forget as long as I live."

The months moved swiftly and Anna's third years at work and at the business college were drawing to a close. She had to pass a final exam at school and studying took all her spare time, as work took up all of her daytime hours. Miss Wagner was not only her boss, she now acted as a tutor, giving Anna tips and information she would need to know for the exam.

The exam was an oral exam by thirteen professors from all across

Europe. Being a shy person, Anna was scared to face these highly educated people. She shouldn't have worried. She scored number two out of fifty-two students. Graduation in itself was not a monumental event. There were no diplomas or long speeches. This time there was praise, but it came from Miss Wagner, not her family. Anna said it seemed to be just the opposite. Now sixteen years old, her family, except for her sister, Johanna, seemed to have deserted her. Instead of being proud of her accomplishments, the rest of the family seemed to be jealous. She had proven to herself and others that she could accomplish what she had set her mind to do.

"Wasn't it worth all that hard work?" Miss Wagner asked Anna.

Anna agreed, especially when her pay increased from ten marks to fifty marks a week. She was now making twenty-five dollars a week. It was a lot of money to this sixteen-year-old.

It was the holiday season once again. The last Sunday in November was the first Advent Sunday. That meant that the flower business was at its peak. Almost everyone ordered Advent wreaths. Advent wreaths were made from blue spruce boughs, holly berries and poinsettia. There were four candles in the wreath, to be lit one at a time moving towards Christmas. Anna and Miss Wagner were now working until midnight many nights to prepare for the next day's business. It was not unusual to make one-hundred-twenty wreaths a day. Their hands took a beating, getting raw and bloody from pine needles and the wire used to put the wreaths together, but this did not seem to slow them down.

Anna dearly loved the Advent Season and Christmas. She felt it was a special time when she felt closer to God. It still bothers her that many people forget the true meaning of Christmas and how precious and holy that season is.

"I always felt like a thousand tiny bells were ringing in my heart," she said. "Because of my long hours at work, I hardly had time to do any Christmas shopping for Mother or my brothers and sisters."

Anna was now able to keep some of what she earned. She still gave her mother one hundred marks each month, but she now had money she could spend for gifts.

As Christmas drew near, the stores announced they would stay open the last two Sundays before Christmas. Anna had some time off on those Sundays and she told her mother she was going shopping. She told her Miss Wagner had given her the afternoon off so she could do her shopping.

Her mother immediately objected. Angry for some unknown reason, she told Anna she couldn't go.

"But I must go," Anna said. "Next Sunday will be too late and besides I have to work in the shop. This is my only chance to buy gifts."

The argument raged. Despite Anna's pleas, her mother said, "NO! You cannot go, and if you do go, the door will be locked when you get back, and you need not come home."

Anna did not understand why her mother was so adamant about not wanting her to go shopping. In fact, at the time she did not take her mother seriously. Still trying some way to please her mother, Anna's main intent was to buy her a nice gift.

Tragically, Anna's good intentions did not pay dividends.

Chapter Eight

It was a beautiful afternoon for shopping in Munich. There were Christmas decorations everywhere. Carols played in the department stores. People shopping and getting ready for the holidays filled the aisles. Signs and sounds of Christmas were everywhere, and Anna was a part of it.

First on her list was her mother. She looked and looked until she found just the right robe, something her mother had needed for a long time, but could not afford with seven children to feed and clothe. Before the afternoon ended, Anna had spent all the cash that she had. After purchasing the robe, she found gifts for her six siblings. This was the first time she ever had money to buy gifts for her family. Full of happiness and joy, her arms loaded down with packages, Anna started toward home. Snow was falling as she waited for the bus. She had a thirty-minute walk after the bus ride, but nothing was going to take the Christmas spirit from her. She sang carols as she trudged along with her packages. It was a happy time.

Climbing the stairs to their apartment, her arms loaded and still singing carols, she rang the doorbell, so someone could help her in. That is when the happiness ended.

No one answered. She rang a second time. No one answered. She went downstairs and started ringing doorbells of other tenants. She needed to put her packages down. She was tired. Finally, a woman on the first floor answered her door and let Anna in. After resting a few moments, she climbed the stairs to try again.

This time, when she reached their apartment door, it finally struck her that her mother had been serious. There, outside the door was a small bundle. It was her clothes. Her mother had not been joking. Her mother locked her out of her own home. She rang the bell three more times, hoping her mother would relent, but there was no answer. She picked up the bundle of clothes, and replaced it with her bags of gifts. She had no idea where to go, or what to do.

For several hours she walked, trying to figure out what to do. The December cold was bitter. Her fingers grew stiff with the cold. Her lips turned blue. Every breath she took let out a steam-like vapor. A few hours ago, her heart was full of joy as she sang Christmas Carols, heading home with gifts for the family. Now she suffered from the bitter cold. She had no place to go. Visions of a hot meal and a warm bed plagued her mind. As the night grew late, lights in the homes she walked by, were turned out. Everyone else was going to bed, making her yearn for her own bed.

She walked until she finally came to a park. At the top of the hill in that park was a bench. In the summertime, lilacs surrounded the bench. Now snow covered the bench and everything around it.

Anna had been here many times before. It had served as her haven when she needed a place to be alone and to think. Now she was back, but this time things were different. There didn't seem to be any solution to this problem.

Her strength was gone. She was as tired as she had ever been in her life. Finally, she gave in. The bench became her bed. Wrapping her coat tightly around her she finally went to sleep. At six a.m., she stumbled to her feet. Stretching and rubbing her eyes, she set out to go to work.

She did not discuss her problems or her situation with her boss. She worked as late that evening as she could, so she could stay in the warm environment. Finally, she returned to her bench in the park for another night of freezing cold. By the third day, she was ill. She arrived at work, and as the day progressed she felt worse and worse. She now suffered from chills. Miss Wagner knew something was wrong with her and expressed her concern.

"I'll fix you a cup of hot tea," she said. "Drink that Anna and then you go home and stay in bed a few days. I can manage alone as long as you can be back by next week. There are only ten more days until Christmas and we are going to be busy."

Anna broke down and cried. She had no home. Finally, she decided she must tell Miss Wagner what had happened. Miss Wagner's first reaction was shock, which quickly turned to anger at Anna for not telling her sooner.

"There is a rollaway bed in the back. There is not much room, but at least you can lie down where it is warm. In the meantime I will find you a room where you can live." Miss Wagner now became her nurse as well as her boss. After two cups of hot tea, Anna fell asleep.

"It was like heaven," she said. "That warm feather bed. It didn't take long to go to sleep. I stayed in bed for two days. Miss Wagner took good care of me and by the third day I was on my feet and back to work."

They soon found one of their customers who had a room to rent. It was nothing fancy but at least Anna had a roof over her head and was out of the snow and cold. The rent took a huge chunk out of Anna's paycheck. The one-hundred marks seemed like a lot of money, but Anna was grateful for a place to stay. She realized that at age sixteen she was now on her own. It was different from living with six siblings and her mother. She said, "As long as I was at work and on the job, I was fine. But in the evening when it was time to close the shop and time for me to go home I became incredibly lonely. I wilted like a flower without water. My room was depressing. There was nothing in it but a bed, a closet to hang my clothes and a square wooden table with one chair. There were no pots or pans. There was one set of linens, which I had to wash and dry there in the room. It was a cold, cheerless room with no heat. I went to bed as soon as I got to my room."

As soon as she had a little money, she bought a portable stove. It was just big enough to heat a bowl of hot soup in the evening and brew a cup of hot tea in the morning.

Anna continued to send money home. Some of her sisters were now working in a factory, but she knew things were still tight for her mother and the family. She never received any thanks and none of the family tried to communicate with her at the shop.

The Christmas rush kept her busy for the next several days. The shop was very busy as customers ordered flowers to decorate their own homes or to give as gifts. The work kept Anna busy every day until after midnight, including the last Saturday and Sunday before the big holiday. By six o'clock on Christmas Eve, business had slowed down. At eight-thirty Miss Wagner locked the door and left to spend the holiday with her sisters. The two women wished each other a "Merry Christmas" and left for their respective homes.

Anna felt exhausted. She had worked hard for several days, but part of her tiredness came from the dread of being alone for Christmas. Her room was bitter cold. With her fingernails, she could literally scrape ice off the walls in her room. Snow was falling, and for a while, Anna just sat and watched the snow from her window. It reminded her of when she was little. Memories of home caused her to start crying. Because of the long hours at work, she had not had time to buy groceries, and she realized that now all the stores were closed.

"I was so hungry," she told me, "that I bit pieces off of two candles I had in my room. I was so cold that I went to bed with my clothes on. As I cried, I started singing Silent Night, Holy Night. I had never felt so lonely in all of my life.

She lit what was left of the two candles, hoping to get a little warmth, and as the wax melted she ate a little more of it hoping to assuage her hunger. Finally, she could stand it no longer. At little after ten p.m. on that Christmas Eve, she rolled out of bed, put on her coat, and braving the twenty-degree weather, she took a streetcar to the neighborhood where her family lived. They had always celebrated Christmas Eve at midnight.

On that night, they had an unknown visitor. A few minutes after midnight, she arrived and walked around the outside of the apartment house. The living room window faced the street and she got an occasional glimpse of family members as they walked by that window.

"I was too scared to ring the bell," she told me. "But I hoped to get a glimpse of the Christmas tree. Every now and then, I could see one of my sisters walking by the window. I heard them laughing and I wondered if they missed me as much as I missed them. I don't recall how long I stood there in the snow. I felt like a thief, hiding so no one would see me. I finally returned to my cold and lonely room. Since I had eaten nothing all day I ate another candle and as I cried I once again called out, 'God, hold me while I cry.'"

Christmas day was to be another day of loneliness. Anna spent much of the day in the feather bed, trying to stay warm, but as evening came, she was restless and hungry. She dressed and decided to do some window-shopping and try to find something to eat. Her shyness kept her from going into a restaurant, something she had never done. She found a bratwurst stand on the street and that is where she had her Christmas dinner.

As she continued walking, she came to a movie theater. On impulse, she purchased a ticket and walked in. The movie was not scheduled to start for an hour, and she spent the time in the waiting area watching the other people as they came in, soon filling the area. Her eyes fell on a "handsome man" who seemed to be paying as much attention to her as she was to him. His attention was a little disconcerting and she finally went to the lady's room to brush her hair. She said that in a way she hoped he would be gone when she got back, but then again, she hoped he was still there.

As she walked up the stairs, he stood on the top step where she could not avoid him.

"Thought I had lost you," he said with a friendly smile. He put out his hand and said, "My name is Rudi." Anna introduced herself and they chatted for a few minutes before he asked her to give him her ticket. As he took her ticket, he said, "Be right back." He quickly returned and handed the ticket to her and she wondered what was going on. As they entered the theater, she found out. The usher led the two of them to adjoining seats. She was happy to not have to sit alone, and even happier when the movie ended and he asked her to have dinner with him.

He took her to a nice restaurant with candles on the tables and soft music for entertainment and according to Anna, "The food was outstanding. I had never been in a place like that. It was a wonderful.evening. I thought to myself, *I'm having Christmas after all.* I hated for the evening to end."

It was past one a.m. when Rudi drove her home in his pickup truck. But he would be back. The two of them became good friends. He waited each evening for her to get off work, not matter how late she was. He was a good listener as she told him of her family situation. But the friendship would not last long.

As they learned more about each other, Anna was startled to find out that Rudi was thirty-six years old, a divorcee with a ten-year-old daughter. Then, when he picked her up one evening and drove to a small café, he startled her even more. As they drank coffee and talked, Rudi blurted out, "Anna, I want to marry you." Anna's coffee cup hit the table and coffee spilled all over her clothes, as her face turned red.

"I appreciate and enjoy your friendship, Rudi, but I'm not ready to get married. I am a long ways from making that kind of commitment."

"I don't expect an answer right away," he replied. Then he left Anna in the café and she went home by herself.

As the days went by without Rudi, she would come home to her empty and lonely room. She spent hours thinking about their relationship. She was still very young. The more she thought about it the more she realized she could not see herself marrying Rudi. As she continued the thought process, she recognized that Rudi had one big problem. He was very possessive and very jealous. She realized that every time a man had looked at her or talked with her, Rudi got upset. He never wanted her to do anything without him. One weekend she had gone to a movie by herself. When she came out of the theater, he stood there waiting for her, angry that she had gone without him. Every evening, without fail, he would be waiting for her when she got off work.

Her conclusion was that she needed to stop seeing him. His desire for a wife and for a mother for his ten-year-old daughter was way too much for a sixteen-year-old girl, still a child herself.

She said, "I wanted a home someday, but I was not ready for marriage. She phoned Rudi and told him she thought it best that they didn't see each other any more. Rudi wasn't ready to give up. He wouldn't take no for an answer. He made the situation very difficult. He insisted on seeing her and then when they were together, he would argue with her constantly, while she hoped that he would just go away.

One evening, as she walked home from work, Rudi pulled up alongside her in his truck. "Get in the car," he said, "I want to talk to you." At first she refused, but he persisted and people on the street were beginning to notice, so, she finally relented. From there things got worse. He demanded to know why she wouldn't marry him. When she tried to explain that their age difference made it impossible when she was only sixteen, he became angrier and angrier. He accelerated and drove down the street like a mad man. Anna grabbed the door handle, scared to death. She thought of jumping out of the moving vehicle. Then he started slapping her. Without warning, he reached across and beat on her as he steered the truck with his other hand. Then he suddenly jammed on the brakes, screeching to a stop, pushed her door open, threw her out of the truck and drove away.

Petrified, Anna started running, afraid he might come back and do her more harm. She soon realized that his blows to her head had caused her nose and moth to bleed. Blood covered her clothes. Her appearance was so embarrassing she would not take the bus home. She walked for an hour and a half to reach her room.

Rudi made one more effort a few days later, when he called to apologize and asked to patch things up, but Anna had enough. That is where the relationship ended.

Anna would soon see other changes in her life, including a serious illness.

Chapter Nine

The next March, in 1956, Anna changed jobs, hoping to better herself. Miss Wagner and Anna had become close friends, almost like mother and daughter, but Anna knew she needed additional experience if she was to move ahead in the business. Her goal was to earn a Master Florist degree.

Mr. & Mrs. Hellreigel were friends of Miss Wagner. They also owned a flower shop, which was extremely busy, and they told Miss Wagner they were desperately in need of help. Mr. Hellreigel was considerably older than his wife, who had many of the symptoms of being bipolar. One day she was all sweetness and light, the next day she was like an ogre. She was extremely jealous, to the point that she did not want her husband or the help to engage in conversation with the customers. It was a good thing that Mr. Hellreigel was a very calm man. Anna said that after working for Mrs. Hellreigel a while, she understood why they were desperate for help. Even after she left the shop, if Mrs. Hellreigel spotted her outside talking with a customer on the street or at the bus stop, the next day Mrs. Hellreigel bawled her out. Then she would punish Anna by putting her to work in the basement where there was no electricity, only candlelight to work by. Anna said that summer or winter, it was always cold in that basement room, and after working by candlelight all day, it was hard to get used to the light when she came out of the dungeon.

Anna had agreed to work for them for a certain length of time. After she realized what she had gotten into, she started counting the days until their agreement ended. With one week left on their agreement, Anna chose a unique way to finish out her time with the Hellreigels.

On her way home from work, she became very ill. Dizziness and nausea struck her down. The next thing she knew, she was in a hospital bed with a very serious kidney infection. Twelve patients, most of them between sixty and eighty years old, occupied her hospital room. Anna was seventeen. Someone in the room died almost every night. The doctors and nurses were very kind to Anna, the bed was warm and comfortable, and the food was good, but it was very depressing to see so many people die. Anna provided the entertainment. Each evening after the nurse turned the lights out, she sat up in bed and sang or yodeled for them until they fell asleep.

Bavaria where Munich is located was once a country of its own and yodeling is a talent unique to Bavarians and the Swiss.

Someone told Anna that the patients in the next ward could also hear her and enjoyed the entertainment. Unfortunately, it came to an abrupt halt when the doctors discovered Anna needed a tonsillectomy. And this, you won't believe.

Anna said it was one of the worst days of her live, one she will never forget. I have never heard of this before, but Anna said they removed her tonsils while she was standing up, with a nurse on each side of her to hold her. The doctor told her to hold her mouth open while he gave her several shots in the back of her throat. Then he told her to take deep breaths while he removed her tonsils. With blood running down her throat, she became extremely sick at her stomach.

She said, "Suddenly, I couldn't swallow any more blood. It all came right up and into the doctor's face. I remember seeing the surprised expression on the doctor's face. Then I passed out. When I regained consciousness I was sitting in a chair, my tonsils were gone. The doctor had finished, whether he wanted to or not, with me sitting in a chair. For three days I wasn't allowed out of bed, and I could not eat or drink."

With nothing else to do, Anna started to reminisce. She thought a lot about her mother. The lack of a relationship with her mother bothered her and the more she thought about it the lonelier and more homesick she became.

One of the other patients had a writing pad and a pen, which Anna was able to borrow. She wrote her mother a letter telling her that she would very much like her mother to come and see her.

"I waited patiently every day," she said, "and when it was time for visiting hours, my heart would beat faster in anticipation. Every day the room would fill with visitors, but no one ever came to see me. Luckily, my bed was the last one by the window, so I could turn my head and cry without anyone seeing me. Crying and being depressed didn't help matters at all, but I couldn't help it."

Kidney problems and the tonsillectomy kept Anna in the hospital for many days. On the tenth day after the tonsillectomy, she had a difficult time going to sleep. Early in the morning around four a.m., she felt something running down her throat. It rapidly became worse and Anna didn't know what to do. The room was dark and she didn't want to wake the other patients. In the dark, she couldn't find the call button to summon the nurse. Then she began to vomit. She desperately needed help, but she couldn't find the call button. Suddenly, the lights came on, and even though it was only a little after four a.m. the day nurse came in and went directly over to Anna's bed. She looked down, gasped and then started to scream.

"Oh, my God," she yelled and ran out screaming for the doctor.

All of the trauma Anna had suffered had manifested itself in a severe hemorrhage in her throat. She lost a large amount of blood before they stopped it, and then Anna had to have several transfusions.

After they treated her and got everything settled down, the nurse who had found her, came back, sat beside Anna's bed, and talked with her.

"I can't believe it," she said repeatedly. "I was home in bed. I had a dream about you, Anna, that you were very ill and needed immediate attention. It is just a dream, I kept telling myself and I tried to go back to sleep. As hard as I tried I couldn't sleep. The more I thought about you, the more worried I became, so I came to the hospital even though I am on the daytime shift. I wanted to check on you, just to be sure. Thank God I came."

Anna also thanked God. She realized that this nurse's dream had saved her life,

Her stay at the hospital continued, and Anna's depression along with it. Five weeks of tests and treatment, and Anna was once again overwhelmed with loneliness. Thoughts of her mother persisted. Anna rued the day she had gone Christmas shopping after her mother had ordered her not to do so. She thought, *Mother won't come to see me because she is still mad at me. I should have never gone shopping against her wishes.*

As quite often happens with depression, thoughts came into her mind, that maybe she wasn't really one of her mother's children. Her mother had never told her she loved her. She remembered when she was young and she would try to put her arms around her mother, only to be pushed away and told, "Don't do that." Anna yearned for some warmth and tenderness from her mother, or anyone else. Writing the note to her mother had not accomplished anything. *Surely she received my letter. She just doesn't care about seeing me, and I have to accept that in my heart.*

One afternoon she stood looking out the window by her bedside. The window overlooked a very pretty park and Anna could see other patients taking slow walks around the park or sitting on benches enjoying the out-of-doors. Anna realized how much she had missed being outside during her long stay at the hospital and she asked permission to go outside and sit in the park for a little while.

With permission given, Anna found a bench not too far from the entrance to the hospital and sat enjoying the sunshine and fresh air.

As she watched people coming and going from the hospital, she suddenly spied a red Volkswagen, which looked very much like one her Aunt Anna had driven the last time she had seen her. She watched carefully as the car pulled into the parking area and stopped. Sure enough, her aunt exited the car and Anna was ecstatic. At last someone was coming to see her. Anna scrambled to her feet and moving as fast as she could, she went to greet her aunt. As she headed toward the car, the passenger door opened and her ninety-eight-year-old grandmother got out. Now, Anna was really excited. Both her aunt and her grandmother were coming to see her.

Wrong. Grandma, in her waning years needed medical care in the hospital for the first time in her life. They had not come to see Anna. In fact, her aunt was completely involved in calming Grandma down who was not at all excited about a stay in the hospital. Anna never knew if they had not known of her hospitalization, and if they knew, if they intended to see her. Crushed once again, Anna returned to her room.

As she lay there thinking about her family, for the first time in weeks, she thought about her dad. Anna had met his new wife a few times, but there had been very little communication between them. Desperate for someone to talk to, she penned a note and gave it to the nurse to mail. After she gave the letter to the nurse, she had second thoughts about contacting her dad and wondered if she had done the right thing. No matter, the letter was on its way and could not be recalled.

The next morning, Anna walked around the room visiting with all of her elderly neighbors. Being the youngest in the room, she found all of them concerned about her and they seemed happy that at last she was able to get up and around to visit with them. After lunch, they all worked at tidying up the space around their beds as they waited for visitors.

When visiting hours arrived, one of the first people into the room was Anna's dad. She said, "He was big and tall and distinguished looking."

Anna was so happy to have a visitor she practically screamed, "Daddy. You came."

Her Dad did something her mother had never done. He held her in his arms for a long time. Then he settled in and visited for the rest of the visiting hours. Anna said they had lots to talk about as they brought each other up-to-date. She said, "I hated for evening to come. It felt so good to have my dad there with me. I could see in his eyes that he really loved me. When he finally left, he promised to come back the next day. How well I remember that night. Joy filled my heart. For the first time in a long time, I was able to sing again. Before I went to sleep, I had a long conversation with God-thanking him over and over again. I knew that God had not forsaken me."

The next day, when her dad returned, he brought his wife, Kathy, with him. She brought all kinds of goodies for Anna. This included a pretty nightgown and a new robe, things Anna really needed. Anna said that it almost seemed like Christmas. Kathy told her that she had wanted to come as soon as they received Anna's note, but Anna's dad said he wanted to come alone the first time and spend a few hours with her. Anna was thrilled. She liked Kathy. Her dad seemed happy and for Anna, that was all that mattered.

It took a two-month hospital stay for Anna to recuperate from her kidney and tonsil problems. She returned to her lonely little room. Miss Wagner came every other day to see how Anna was doing and to bring food. A good friend, she did her best to take care of her former employee, even becoming her employment agency.

"How would you like to work with a Florist-Master in Garmish-Partenkirchen?" she asked Anna one evening when she stopped by. "There is a job there for you and I think you will like it, since I know how much you enjoy your work."

Anna was thrilled. She said, 'It was like a dream come true." She was to work with a man who was a Master Florist, and this in itself was an honor. A week later she left Munich and went to work in Garmish-Partenkirchen, which is a town south of Munich and right in the Alps. She found lodging in an Almshouse, a home for those who were struggling financially. Josef was the Master Florist and Anna said he was a good teacher who really knew and loved his work. She said that in six months of training and working with him, she learned more than she had learned in the past three years. The other employees were kind to her, and she enjoyed the work so much that she didn't mind the late hours required of her. Once a week those hours were very long. Every Friday they redecorated their showroom window and that job took until two a.m. "It was fun," she said, "We all worked together like a family. For the first time I enjoyed going home after my long days of work."

Living there was true Alpine living. At five a.m. a herd of cows with their bells clanging around their necks, walked down the street in front of Anna's bedroom window, on their way to pasture. Many mornings she could leave her window open and enjoy the fresh mountain air. The view of the Alps was magnificent. Anna said she thanked God each day for the opportunity to live and work in such a beautiful atmosphere. Every opportunity she had for a day off, and on the weekends, she hiked in the mountains, learning to use Alpine equipment, heavy soled shoes and ropes. She reveled in the beauty of the mountains and in the danger that came with climbing.

At the same time, she applied herself to her work and on September 23, 1958, at the age of nineteen, she received her Master Florist Degree. This meant a substantial increase in her income and job offers to consider. When she wrote Miss Wagner and told her of her accomplishments, her former mentor shared in her excitement and happiness.

Perhaps the most pleasant news was a letter from Anna's mother. Anna had continued to send home half of her earnings, because she felt her mother needed the money and Anna had learned to live on half of what she made. Shortly after receiving her designation as a Master Florist, a long letter came from Mama, congratulating Anna. It was the first time in six years that she had contact with her mother. Because it had been so long and because her mother had never shown Anna any affection, she was a little hesitant to open the letter, but was happy to find a congratulatory comment from her mother as well as some brief news about what was going on at home. She found out that her sister Johanna had been married for five years, Renate had been married for two years and had a new baby boy.

Her mother's letter moved Anna to want to visit home. She didn't write, The next weekend she took the train to Munich. Along the way, she had second thoughts. She wondered how she would be received, if coming home like this was the right thing to do. She realized that just seeing Munich again was worth the risk. That was her home, and she was thrilled to be back.

As she neared their home, some of the neighbors recognized her and greeted her. They seemed as happy to see her as she was to once again see her home. She thought, *If only Mother is as happy to see me as I am to be here.*

"I was almost afraid to ring the doorbell," she said. "But when I did, my youngest sister, Tilly, opened the door, said 'What do you want?' and closed the door in my face."

It was obvious that Anna's mother had influenced the way her sister felt.

"I was shocked," she said. "For a moment I just stood there. Then, I picked up my little suitcase and started to leave. Just then I heard Mother call my name. I turned around and went back. She greeted me with a handshake and asked me to come in. I was almost in tears. We sat down and had a cup of tea together and talked for an hour."

Her mother than took her to Renate's house so she could see her new nephew. Anna was pleased to see the cute baby, Eddi, and then received a pleasant surprise.

Renate said, "Sunday is Eddi's christening and I haven't chosen a Godmother yet."

"What about me?" Anna asked.

Renate said, "Yes. I would be more than happy if you want to be his Godmother." Anna said she did not feel that Renate was as happy about it as she was.

Anna commented that, "It was good to be part of the family again. I spent a peaceful weekend with them, except for Tilly, who made it very plain that she was not too happy with my being there."

As Anna rode the train back to Garmish-Partenkirchen, she reflected on her visit, realizing that she was much happier to see her family than they seemed to see her. "I loved my family dearly. Never once did I feel that they felt anything for me, but still my heart cried out to all of them. When love comes from the heart, it is there to stay, no matter what. I was so glad to have seen Mother again. In a way I believed she had been happy to see me to, but wouldn't admit it."

Her mother did not hug or kiss Anna, but Anna felt that they had made some progress because her mother did smile at her and took time to talk with her.

The following week, as she worked, Anna could not help but think about the previous weekend. She worried about the coolness of her sisters towards her, and the fact that her mother still did not show any affection to her.

Then she realized, "I have a good job and my own life to live. I send money home every week. What more could I do?"

As the Christmas season approached, Anna and her co-workers were once again overwhelmed with work. A famous Bavarian hotel, the Alpenhof was right next door to the florist shop. Every weekend during the holidays they had big events scheduled, and particularly on the Friday evening before Christmas. That night the guests were movie stars and important business people and Josef's Flower Shop was in charge of the décor. After they completed the decorations, Josef appointed Anna to be the flower girl. She welcomed everyone, pinning pink orchid corsages on each woman and red carnations on the men. Then Anna spent the rest of the evening selling the remainder of her corsages to other guests of the hotel. It was an exciting evening for this young woman who had not had many opportunities for excitement in her life.

She was still working at two a.m. as the parties began to break up. Many of the guests had imbibed in the alcohol beverages to the point that some of them were singing in the lobby, while others had passed out on the couches. After such a long day, Anna was tired when her boss Josef Kurht called all the employees together. They met in the bar where he offered them a drink before they went home. Anna said she was so tired, that all she wanted to do was go home, but she felt obligated to stay for a moment and visit with the others as they had their drinks. Suddenly, she realized that the bartender kept looking at her.

As their eyes met, he introduced himself. "I'm Peter. Who are you?"

"I'm the florist from next door," she told him.

"I haven't seen you before. Are you new?"

"No. I've worked her for almost eighteen months."

Peter had gotten her attention. He was dark haired and handsome and she liked him from the start as he was friendly and seemed like a gentleman. Their conversation continued for quite some time, and Anna realized that she was no longer tired. As the last patrons left the bar, and everything shut down for the night, Peter asked Anna if he could see her the next day, for a movie and perhaps dinner.

She agreed and so the next day they had their first date. She found that they had many similar interests including mountain climbing. Whenever they had some free time, they enjoyed climbing together. At four a.m. on the weekends, they would start climbing and not return until dark. Unless you are familiar with the Alps the names won't mean much, but they climbed Zugspits twice, Rothwand, Konigstand, Ross, Buchstein and others. They joined a climbing club where they met many other climbers and Anna said, "We had lots of fun. The Alps are breathtaking, especially in the winter when the peaks are crowned with snow. Peter and I had mountain climbing fever all year long, summer and winter. We took long walks in the clean, fresh air and in the green pastures with the prettiest flowers nature could provide. I loved every minute of it, and thought what a blessing God gave us when he gave us eyes to see all of the beauty."

Their friendship continued for almost a year. Then one Sunday afternoon, as they walked through some green pastures, enjoying the beauty around them, Peter put his arm around Anna and kissed her. Until that moment, they had just been friends. Now, Peter told her that he had wanted to kiss her for a long time, but he wasn't sure how she felt. She told him quickly that she felt the same as he did, that life was more beautiful than ever, that she was in love for the very first time.

Anna was on cloud nine. She had found someone who cared about her, wanted to spend time with her, said that he loved her, words she had not heard from her own family. Peter shared information about his family and what they did. His father was Will Domgraf Fassbaender, a famous opera singer. His aunts and uncles were also opera singers. They were all people who made their living on the stage, known for their beautiful and gifted voices.

Peter then admitted, "Unfortunately, I can't carry a tune, no matter how hard I try. I'm just not cut out for that. So I became a bartender." That comment provided them with a few laughs.

Then the romance was interrupted. Peter's company transferred him to England for a new assignment. Anna was very unhappy to see him leave. She could not imagine life without Peter. At the same time, he was excited about the new opportunity, because he was to be given some business training, enabling him to be promoted to a better position.

Anna realized that it was important for Peter and that it was only a one-year assignment. She kept busy with her work, hoping the time would pass quickly. Evenings by herself were long and lonely without him. He corresponded every other day with her, but she still missed him. Finally, the year came to an end.

It was just a matter of weeks until he would be back. His letters had kept Anna's spirits up, and she was anxious for his return. Then came a very special letter.

"Peter asked me to marry him as soon as he returned," she told me. "In three more weeks, I'll be home, Angel," he wrote.

She read the letter over and over and then later that evening she wrote to Peter, telling him how happy she was that she was going to spend her life with him.

Her co-workers shared in her joy. She began looking for a place for them to live and soon found a nice furnished apartment, "just perfect for Peter and me."

The day grew nearer and the time seemed to pass very slowly. She wrote and told him about the apartment. "We can move in as soon as we are married," she told him.

He wrote back, "Just a few more days. I have had enough of England. I am looking forward to coming home and to be with you."

The days passed and Peter was finally due home, but he didn't arrive. Not only that, there were no more letters. Anna became very concerned. She wrote to him again, and the letter came back unopened, and marked, "MOVED." Now, Anna was very upset. She didn't know what to think. It was hard to go to work and concentrate on what she was doing, when she had no idea of what had happened to Peter. She asked herself repeatedly, *What has happened to him? Where can he be?*

Three weeks went by and there was no word. Not wanting to be alone for the weekend, she went to the florist shop to work, even though she was not scheduled. It was a very busy Sunday afternoon. The shop was usually crowded with people, and this day was no exception. As the time came to close, another customer walked in. Anna quickly waited on her, knowing everyone was ready to leave. The customer picked out a beautiful flowerpot. Anna realized they had run out of wrapping paper, so she picked up some newspaper to wrap the pot in. As she started to wrap the pot, her eyes caught the headline about a car accident. As she looked closer, she said, "I suddenly felt like every drop of blood was draining out of my body. Underneath the headlines, it said in big print, 'William Domgraf Fassbaender's Son Killed in Car Accident.' I wasn't able to finish reading the story. I suddenly knew that Peter was dead. Now, everything became clear. Peter's death was a shock. The man I loved was dead. My dreams were shattered into pieces. My world fell apart."

Anna tried to bury herself in her work. She said she worked harder and longer hours than ever before. Sometimes on a pretty, sunshiny day, she would walk up into the mountains but her interest in mountain climbing had waned. She said, "Without Peter, nothing seemed to be the same. I walked and walked to all the special places Peter and I used to sit. For hours I talked to God and asked him, 'Why, God?' But He didn't seem to answer.

I cried many tears, but life went on and the only choice I had was to put the pieces of my life back together no matter how hard it was."

She never heard a word from anyone in Peter's family and had no way of knowing if they even knew about her.

Within a short period of time, Anna decided she could not continue to stay there with memories of Peter. She quit her job, and purchased a one-way ticket to Munich. It was time to go home and see her mother again. Anna felt a great need for her mother to comfort her. It was a weekday, and the train was almost empty. As the train moved farther from the mountains, Anna's emotions enveloped her as she said goodbye to this place she had come to love. She had such good memories of mountain climbing with Peter, the beauty of the Alps, and the shop where she had learned so much about her profession.

She arrived in Munich around noon, and before going home, she decided to visit Miss Wagner. She was welcomed home and the two sat and drank several cups of tea and talked for almost two hours. It was good to be back in Munich.

Her reception at home was not what she desired. Her mother expressed her surprise in seeing her and her disappointment that Anna had quit her job. Anna had saved a little money, which she gave to her mother and that seemed to calm her to some extent. Anna felt that her mother was mainly upset because now Anna did not have money to send home each week.

She yearned for her mother to just put her arms around her and comfort her. *If only she would tell me she loved me,* Anna thought as she fought to hold the tears back. She assured her mother she would soon have a new job, that she didn't need to worry. Her mother agreed to let her live there for the time being.

Chapter Ten

Anna's first stop the next morning as she started job hunting was to go back to Miss Wagner. The friendship and advice given to her by Miss Wagner meant a lot to Anna. Her former boss also had many contacts and was always willing to help. At the moment, Miss Wagner was in need of help herself. The girl who worked for her was stealing money, and had to be let go. So Anna was back where she had started at age thirteen working for a woman who was not only a good teacher but was very unselfish.

Several weeks passed when news came that 20th Century Fox was opening a movie studio right there in the neighborhood. They contracted with Miss Wagner to provide flowers for their décor and for the movies they made. She asked Anna to take responsibility for this. Excited at a new and different opportunity, Anna loved the work. She had an opportunity to meet many movie stars and the job was very challenging. Unfortunately, the contract only lasted for one year. Miss Wagner chose not to extend the contract. Once again, Anna was looking for work.

At the same time, things were not going well at home. Mama never asked the two sisters still at home to do any chores, although they came from their factory work at five o'clock. When Anna returned home late in the evening, the supper dishes were always waiting for her. Her mother constantly criticized Anna and the friction between the two of them grew. Until, one day it exploded.

Anna had a Saturday off. She did all the chores around the house and late in the afternoon started listening to a story on the radio. Her mother had gone grocery shopping and when she came home and found Anna sitting down listening to the radio, she told her to "Turn that thing off. Don't you have anything better do to?"

"All the work is done," Anna said. "Besides, this story is almost over."

Talking back to Mother was a no-no. Anna's word caused her mother to have a tantrum, almost getting hysterical. Going into the kitchen, she opened the utensil drawer, took out the biggest butcher knife in the drawer and said, "If you say one more word, I'll cut your throat."

This was not the first time she had threatened Anna, and to this day, Anna will tell you with tear-filled eyes, "It was as if I was not one of her daughters."

As the flower job with Twentieth Century ended, Miss Wagner came through again. She had a contact in northern Germany in a town called Baumholder through the wholesale flower deliveryman. Baumholder was located on the Moselle River in grape country. The florist shop there needed help and Miss Wagner arranged for Anna to go there to work. It was a long ways from Bavaria and the Alps. Here the country was more rolling and vineyards filled the hillsides. The accent in their language was even somewhat different. Anna had to pay close attention to what they were saying to enable her to understand. She had been used to speaking Bavarian, but now she had to speak High German. With some trepidation about going to a town she had never heard of to work for people she did not know, Anna boarded the train for a seven-hour ride north. She enjoyed the scenery, but it did not compare to the Alps.

Miss Wagner had drawn Anna a map showing her how to find the shop once she arrived. She received a warm greeting, a thorough tour of the shop and she found that her new employer had even rented a small, furnished apartment for her.

It was a completely new experience.

Anna found that there were a good number of American soldiers stationed near there. She recalled memories of earlier war days, when American troops had taken over their apartment For some reason, those memories provoked a fear in Anna that forced her to spend much of her spare time in her apartment. That fear caused her to panic one afternoon as she walked home from work. She heard a roaring sound which became louder and louder. Suddenly an American tank rolled around the corner, followed by another and another. A whole column of tanks was soon rolling down the streets. Anna turned and ran back to the shop as fast as she could go. Pushing the door open, she yelled, "Another war! Another war!"

Anna was trembling all over. She was almost hysterical. The shop owner called a doctor to give her a sedative. When she had calmed down, he explained that the Americans were often on maneuvers in the area and she would have to get used to it. She told me that those memories from her early childhood still surface. She still cannot watch a war movie or TV show. She says the nightmares of war and concentration camps woke her, screaming, many nights for a long time after the war was over.

Her paranoia about war was very serious to her, but it provided amusement for those she worked with who often kidded her. "I could never live through another war," she said. "I was sure about that. The scars and nightmares were still there after all these years."

As the months passed, Anna got to know the people in Baumholder quite well, becoming friends with some. She found things to do on the weekends when she was off. Dances, concerts, and other activities kept her busy. The woman who owned the shop, and other acquaintances Anna made, often went with her.

A tall American soldier became a daily customer. He spoke German fluently, which enabled them to converse, because Anna knew no English. Every day he bought a few flowers. One afternoon as Anna wrapped his purchase he invited her to go to a movie with him. Anna still had a fear of American soldiers and although he was nice to her, she said, "No." But, he didn't give up. Every day he came back and bought flowers, each time asking her to go out with him.

The woman who owned the shop told Anna, "You have known him long enough. Why not say yes? Accept his invitation. It really can't hurt a thing."

However, it would take a long time and a lot of misery for Anna to realize her boss gave her some bad advice.

It took a little more time for Anna to be convinced but she finally agreed to go with Jack to an American movie. Not knowing any English, Bali Hai was a movie Anna would have a difficult time to understand, but she said, "I kind of put two and two together."

After the movie, they went to the NCO Club for dinner. Jack introduced her to some of his friends and she enjoyed the evening, learning a few words of English in the process

Sergeant Jack Pearce was originally from Dallas and now called Houston home. He was 6'4" tall with dark hair. He was a tank commander who had served in Korea.

Their dates became more frequent and Anna began to feel more secure about being with an American soldier. One of Jack's friends, a soldier Anna knew as Jim, married a German girl and they invited Anna and Jack to the wedding, with Jack to be Jim's best man. Jim's bride, Erika asked Anna to be her maid of honor. Not surprisingly, that same evening Jack asked Anna to marry him. She said yes and so, that same evening, they celebrated their engagement. There was quite a bit of paperwork to complete for them to be married and it had to be completed in both English and German. It took six months to get the forms prepared. Then Jack brought them to Anna for her signature. At that point she got cold feet. She decided she needed more time. This irritated Jack, but Anna insisted on waiting.

Anna began to pay more attention to Jack's habits. She realized he drank liquor quite often and quite heavily. She told him she did not like drinking and his answer was that he drank because there was nothing else to do. "If I was married, and had a family I wouldn't have any reason to drink."

This had some logic in Anna's thinking and she believed him. In the meantime, she burned the papers and told Jack she didn't know where they were. He started the process again and five months later produced a new set. This time she felt obligated to sign them. Something inside her told her, *Anna, you are making a big mistake.*

As the news of the upcoming wedding spread around the small town, Anna's German friends told her she was making a mistake to marry a G.I. A young German named Helmut, even confessed his attraction to her and offered to marry her. He was quite upset that she was considering marrying Jack.

Anna missed Jack's company when he was on maneuvers. She felt that she was in love with him. Finally, the date was set. This caused her German friends to shun her, particularly the men, who asked, "Aren't we good enough for you?" The women just ignored her.

Even this didn't bother Anna, as much as the thought of telling her mother. She decided to break the news to her mother in a letter and the reply she received was not congratulatory. "Have you forgotten the war and how the Americans treated us? And now, you are going to marry one of them? As far as I am concerned I no longer have a daughter, and you won't ever set foot in this household again."

A not too unexpected reaction from a mother who had never shown Anna any love or concern. The result seemed to be a stronger resolve on Anna's part to move on. *Everybody else gets married. So, he is an American. The only difference I see is that he speaks another language. Other than that, he is just like the other men I know.*

February 15 was the day. Anna got up early, cleaned the apartment, mopped the floors, bathed and got dressed for her wedding. It was a cold, snowy day. Erika and Jim, the couple Jack and Anna had stood up for, now returned the favor. They picked Jack up, then came to get Anna and the four of them drove to the courthouse. Anna's wedding gown was a short white velvet dress. The Master Florist realized her groom had not even purchased a wedding bouquet for the brief ceremony. When the time came for Jack to put a ring on her finger, she found that he hadn't purchased one of those either.

"We had waited nearly a year for this day," Anna said, "but he had not taken the time to buy a ring or a bouquet for me. I was hurt and bewildered."

However, disenchantment was just starting to set in. They went from the courthouse to Erika and Jim's apartment for cake and coffee. Erika had decorated the table beautifully. As Anna finished with her first cup of coffee, some of Jack's buddies arrived with a case of whiskey. Anna was upset, but it only got worse. By three o'clock in the afternoon, Jack had passed out from the alcohol. Erika and Jim helped Anna take him to the apartment and put him to bed. The party was over and Anna sat by herself on her wedding night, tears streaming down her cheeks.

She changed from her wedding dress into some warm, comfortable clothes, and went for a walk. The snow was coming down heavily and the fresh, cold air was invigorating, but Anna felt choked up. Her throat was tight. On her wedding night, she had to admit to herself. *I made a mistake.*

She started crying as she continued to walk staying out in the cold for over three hours. "What a wedding day," she said. "I hadn't expected it to be like this, although everyone had warned me. I didn't listen and now it was too late. I turned around and started slowly for home. I didn't really feel like going home, but I was hungry. The only thing I had eaten all day was one piece of cake at Erika's."

Jack was still asleep when she arrived home at eight p.m. Anna made a pot of tea and a sandwich and went to bed. The next morning Jack was all apologies. Although Anna felt that he loved her, his main interest seemed to be alcohol. His army friends had a lot of influence on him. Almost every night they would go drinking and try to drink the others "under the table." Toward the end of the month, he would run out of money and he would not be able to drink for a few nights, but he looked forward to payday. On payday, he often disappeared. He would be gone for a few days, not telling

Anna where he was going. Three days later, he would show up with most of his pay spent.

These were harsh days for Anna. They argued and fought. Jack didn't hesitate to hit her when he got angry. He lost his stripes in the military more than once because of his drinking problem. He was demoted from Sergeant to an SP4, then from SP4 to a PFC. None of this seemed to bother him. It was more like a game to Jack and his pals. Whoever lost his stripes first had to buy the next case of whiskey. That led to more drinking.

Anna had all she could take. They separated, but Jack kept pursuing her, trying to prove that he was a "good man." When he was sober, he would treat her well, but when he was drunk, he beat her and cursed her.

Anna said, "I tried over and over to see his good side. I kept on hoping and praying that one of these days he would give up the drinking. With that hope in my heart, I went back to him. We both tried to make this marriage work. Everything went well, but only until payday."

Realizing that Jack was an alcoholic was one thing. Knowing how to cope with it was something else. This was all new to Anna. She had never been in this kind of a situation before. She made up her mind she had to live with it hoping that the drinking and abuse would somehow miraculously cease.

Anna was twenty-two years old when her doctor told her she was pregnant. She left the doctor's office anxious to share the good news with Jack. Jack had said at one time that if he had a family he would be busy enough that he wouldn't need to drink. Anna now hoped that would be true.

Jack's excitement didn't last long. At six a.m. he would hit the bottle. By ten a.m. on the days he was home, she would find him passed out on the floor. To make matters worse, the violence escalated. He blamed his time in Korea for wanting to "fight and kill" every time he got drunk. He said that in his mind he was in Korea, fighting the war again. When he sobered up the next day, he would see the bruises he had inflicted on Anna and would be deeply apologetic.

Anna became afraid of Jack, terrified when she heard him coming up the stairs to their apartment. She said, "It seemed like he had two personalities. When he wasn't drinking he was a good and gentle man, and we were a happy couple, but when he was drunk and this was most of the time, he was abusive, both mentally and physically. My marriage became a nightmare. I was depressed most of the time and didn't know what to do. I tried to make the best of it, but the situation became worse.

I cried myself to sleep most every night I had no one to turn to. Everyone told me, 'I told you so.'"

When she was six months pregnant, she volunteered to work at the flower shop one evening, just to get out of the house. She was walking slowly, being six months pregnant. Her mind wandered. Suddenly a taxi pulled alongside her. To her dismay, Jack jumped out cursing her for going to work. People along the street could not help but witness the confrontation, which naturally embarrassed Anna. She tried to calm Jack, but the more she said, the angrier he became. Suddenly, he grabbed her by her hair, pulling her off her feet. Then, he proceeded to drag her down the street by her hair, her body.dragging along the street.

She screamed for help. "Thank God, the German police came by and immediately stopped to help me. They handcuffed Jack and held him in their car until the Military Police arrived. As I regained some composure, I realized my legs, arms and hips were skinned and raw. My clothes were bloody. One of the young policemen asked me if I was pregnant and when I told him 'Yes, six months,' he just shook his head in disbelief because of the treatment Jack had given me. The police took me home and Jack spent the night in jail."

Anna spent a restless night, worrying about Jack, and what he would do when they released him. She was puzzled as to why his drinking seemed to get worse and worse. He was beating her almost every day. She found it impossible to live with him and his drinking and temper. But like so many women in that situation she could still see the "good side" in Jack. This happened at the end of each month when he was broke and couldn't buy liquor. When he was sober, they were a happy couple. Unfortunately, those days were very few, and then payday came again.

The next evening Jack was back home. Anna's mind was in turmoil. She didn't know what to do or say. Therefore, she said nothing and Jack did the same. She told me, "I guess he was too ashamed to apologize. This had been no isolated incident. Things like this happened repeatedly. My marriage to Jack was a nightmare. He had big hands, and he hit hard as well as kicked. One time, while I was pregnant, he kicked me in the stomach. "

Meantime, she tried to correspond with her mother, hoping her mother would tell her that she cared for Anna and was willing to help in some way. It was to no avail. Not a word came back from Munich. She felt that she was no longer a member of the family, that they had rejected her. That hurt as much as knowing that her marriage was a failure and that she was taking a tremendous amount of abuse. She was frustrated, not knowing what to do. She wanted to end the marriage, but felt she had alienated the whole town because she had married an American soldier. When she talked of divorce to Jack, he told her he would kill her so no one else could have her. Her summary: "His love, as I saw it, meant possession and domination, not tenderness, gentleness and love."

In her seventh month of pregnancy, the army sent Jack on maneuvers. While he was gone, Anna became very ill. The pain was excruciating. The worst times came when she walked. She couldn't sit down or bend over. The first pains came one evening after the doctor's office had closed. She spent a long, painful night. In tremendous pain, she slowly managed to pack a suitcase. She wanted to scream with every move she made. She felt certain that when she saw the doctor, he would send her to the hospital. Standing still was the only way to alleviate the pain, so she stood by the window, waiting for the sun to rise. When the sun finally appeared around five a.m., she set out with her suitcase to walk to the doctor's office. It took her an hour to get to there, because each step brought a great deal of pain with it. She knew she would be three hours early, but she didn't care. Being first in line was the most important thing.

"Emergency!" the doctor said on the phone after examining her. "I need an ambulance as fast as you can get here." He turned toward Anna, shaking his head negatively. He told here, "We must hurry, or you won't make it through the day."

Anna said, "I did not know what was wrong with me, but I was in so much pain I really didn't care."

The ambulance wasted no time and twenty minutes later Anna was in the Baumholder hospital operating room. The next day, when she woke she realized he pain had receded. "How do you feel," the doctor asked.

"I really don't know. I am still feeling the drugs."

"It is not over yet," he added. "We must operate again in five days."

Then he explained that she had a cyst on her tailbone that had been there since birth and had grown as time went by the pregnancy caused the cyst to burst and gangrene set in and began to spread.

Then he told her his best friend had died from the same thing, before the man could even get to the doctor. He told her, "Just trust me. I will do everything I can."

Anna said, "The doctor was about fifty years old. He reminded me of my father. I did trust him."

The doctor asked about her family and Anna's tears kept her from telling him much. Finally, he said, "Just give me their address. I will write to them."

On the fifth day, Jack had not come back and no one else had been by to see her. Once again, Anna had to face her problems alone. The nurse came in to warn Anna, "We don't know if we can save your baby. I think you should know and be prepared for the worst."

The hospital priest came in to pray with her, and by that, Anna knew that the baby and her own chances were not too good. In the next thirty minutes, Anna had many thoughts about her mother and her siblings. She regretted not having her father's address so she could contact him. She pulled the sheet up over her and wept. She cried out to God, "Oh please, don't let me die." Despite her prayers, she wavered in her thoughts of God as being unreachable, and then of God as her only friend. She called Him her secret friend. With those thoughts in her mind, she went to surgery.

When she woke, her first instinct was to put her hand on her stomach. She was still carrying her baby. As she opened her eyes, she found her favorite nurse and the doctor standing by her bed.

"Everything is over," the doctor told her. You are going to be all right. It will be tough for a few days, but you and your baby are going to be just fine."

They had burned out the cyst after they cut her tailbone to get to it. She was very uncomfortable for several days but happy to be alive and still have her baby.

Anna's recovery took six more weeks. She was finally released and wasn't sure what she would find at home. She had not heard one word from Jack, or anyone else, during her hospital stay. The doctor ordered an ambulance to take her home and she was shocked when she walked in to find the apartment almost empty. Jack was asleep on the sofa with an empty whiskey bottle beside him.

Her first instinct was just to run away, but she calmed herself, walked to the grocery store to buy provisions so she could fix Jack a good meal.

The neighbors were surprised when they saw her. They did not even know she had been in the hospital. Jack didn't know either. When he woke up, he was surprised to find her there. He had just assumed she had left him and he had been on one long drunk after he came back from maneuvers. He had sold most of the furniture to buy whiskey.

Anna felt bad that she hadn't written him a note, and Jack felt bad that he thought she had left him and didn't know that she had faced a near death situation in the hospital. He was so remorseful, he promised never to drink again. He kept the promise, for a while.

Anna was happy. Jack was sober and the time was near for her to have the baby. Five weeks and they would have the addition to their family. Jack went to work each day and came home sober. When his drinking friends invited him out, he turned them down. He wrote to Houston and asked his family for money and they sent enough to tide them over until the next payday. Anna said, "Everything was lovely. Jack and I were once again happy."

Realizing the addition to the family would require more space, Anna went apartment hunting. She soon found a much roomier place. She was anxious for Jack to come home so she could tell him, but the whole base went on maneuvers again. Jack was not there to help her move, so she tackled the job herself. They were moving into the second floor of a home, which Anna described as "Lovely with a terrace, just perfect for the baby."

She used her new baby buggy to move their clothes and household goods. It was February, cold and snowy. By the time she was finished, she was very tired, almost nine months pregnant and climbing stairs at both apartments wore her out..

Jack was due home the next day. She was determined to have the move completed when he arrived. She said, "At three o'clock I was finished. It looked so nice and homey. I was proud of it. I looked in the mirror and my face was pink and rosy. I took a bath and went to bed. Two hours later, I woke with a terrible pain. It didn't last long and I dozed off, but thirty minutes later the same thing happened."

As the pains came more frequently, Anna called for a taxi, but when the pains were down to three minutes apart, the taxi had not arrived. Anna put on a robe and slippers, grabbed her suitcase and walked to the hospital. It had snowed all night long and was now three feet high. Her slippers kept coming off, and between getting them back on and stopping for the labor pains, she had a struggle to get to the hospital. The hospital sat on a hill and the last part of the walk was up that hill. Out of breath, pains coming rapidly, she made it to the door, and found it locked. Fortunately, there was a bell and the night nurse came and opened the door. Shocked at seeing Anna in robe and slippers, she was more astounded when she learned that Anna had walked the entire way. She remembered Anna from her previous stay, and hastened to call the doctor.

Two hours later, on February 2, 1962 Birgitta Pearce was born. Anna was able to reach Jack by phone at the camp and he was excited about being a father. She anxiously waited all day for him to come and see her and the baby. When he appeared late that afternoon, he was drunk.

Anna was devastated. She tried not to say anything, knowing that his excuse would be that he was celebrating the birth of their child, but she was hurt and very afraid that their marriage would again fall apart.

"And I was right," she said. "Jack should never have taken that drink with his friends. He broke his promise to me, and I knew what it would do to him-and to us."

Chapter Eleven

Anna's life changed. Having a baby to care for required some major adjustments, but she also found it fulfilling. With someone else in her life besides Jack, she found that she didn't feel as empty. Birgitta became the center of her life. They spent long periods of time every day walking. She talked to the baby as if she understood. She was able to laugh again, but she also cried as she held the small infant. She had someone to talk to and when the baby smiled and her brown eyes lit up, Anna felt like her heart would melt. "Oh, how she made my life worth living," Anna told me. "I had hoped that his new little daughter would be the turning point in Jack's life, but he actually turned in the opposite direction, spending more time with his drinking pals. He was seldom at home."

Jack's drinking problems became so severe that several times he had to go to the hospital for treatment. The doctor told Anna there was nothing they could do for Jack until he was willing to help himself. When they would talk with Jack about how serious his drinking problem had become, he just laughed at them. He refused to admit that he was an alcoholic. He became angry with everyone and the anger prompted him to drink even more. The whiskey bottle became the most important thing in his life.

Then God stepped in once more. One thing that helped Anna through this was meeting an older German couple who invited her to spend time in their home. They enjoyed having Birgitta there, especially since they had never had children of their own. Anna said that, in a way, they adopted her and the baby. Mother and daughter actually found themselves spending more time with Erika and Klaus than they did at home. It was very depressing at home and Jack had started beating Anna again. Sometimes, late in the evening when Jack started beating her, she would grab the baby and run to Erika and Klaus. She said they always took her in no matter how late it was.

Spring was here and around May 1, Erika and Klaus decided to go to East Berlin to help celebrate Erika's parent's fiftieth wedding anniversary. "I will miss you both," Anna told them. "Three weeks is a long time for me to not have my friends nearby."

Anna went home that afternoon, feeling empty inside. She was going to miss her friends very much, as well as missing the haven they provided her when Jack became violent. This couple had become like family, much more so than her own family had ever been, always being there for Anna when she needed them.

When she arrived home, she put the baby down and started fixing dinner. As she started to set the table, Jack walked in, and with him was a small group of guys ready to party. Anna knew what the evening would be like. Although dinner was ready, Jack refused to eat, which meant he was drinking on an empty stomach. As midnight approached, the party continued. Anna and the baby spent the evening in the bedroom.

She became aware that the partygoers in her living room had raised their voices. As she listened, she realized that an argument had broken out. She walked out to see what the problem was just as dishes started flying. Anna told them to leave, and this made Jack angrier. This was not just an argument, people were being hurt and bloodied. Anna was scared for herself and the baby.

Grabbing Birgitta, Anna left the apartment as quickly and quietly as possible. Once outside and away from the house, she realized that her usual haven, Erika and Klaus would be leaving in the morning for East Berlin. She hesitated to bother them, but she needed somewhere to take the baby, at least until morning. Erika had told her many times that no matter how late it was, the door was always open. So, that is where they went and spent the rest of the night.

Anna cried most of the night. She had worked so hard to fix up their new apartment to have a nice home for Jack and the baby, and Jack and his friends destroyed it all in a couple hours time.

When morning came, she was very hesitant to go home, not knowing what she would find. Erik and Klaus solved the problem, at least temporarily. They invited her and the baby to come with them to East Berlin. Afraid to go home, Anna accepted. She had to go home to get some clothes, but fortunately, Jack was gone. As she expected, the apartment was a mess, littered with broken pieces of furniture and dishes. Anna hurriedly packed what she needed and ran back to Erika's. By mid-morning, they were on their way. Little did she realize that a different kind of adventure awaited them.

Anna said the trip was exciting and breathtaking, with beautiful scenery. Erika's parents welcomed them and Anna found them warm and sincere people. Anna did notice one thing, Erika's parents never laughed. Then, as she became acquainted with others who lived nearby, she found the same thing true with them. They seemed to be afraid to be themselves. There was a fear there that Anna said caused her to wonder why the people of East Berlin were so different from people in West Berlin who were open and humorous. In West Berlin the children ran and played in the streets, but in East Berlin that was not true. Here, the streets were empty and quiet. She continued to take Birgitta for a walk each day, but it was almost like a deserted city. She said that sometimes she felt chills running down her back because the atmosphere was so cold and creepy.

One afternoon she felt like she had someone following her. She could hear the echo of footsteps on the cobblestones. It frightened her enough that she decided to stop taking walks. That same day she received a warning that for political purposes she should not go out alone.

She realized that Erika and Klaus seemed very upset. Erika was in tears. "What's going on here?" Anna asked. "Did I do something wrong?"

"No," Klaus answered. "Something has come up. It is a very difficult situation. We are trapped. Last night the city was divided in half and the Russians will allow no one to enter or leave East Berlin."

The Cold War had started in earnest, and the Russians were exerting their power. Klaus was very concerned because they had asked Anna to come with them, and she was married to an American soldier, which he did not want the Russians to know. The Berlin wall was set up overnight without any warning, and now they were like prisoners there.

For those younger people who don't know the history of Berlin, after World War II, the Russians occupied East Germany. The Allied forces, mainly American and English occupied the West. Russia did not want to cooperate with the others and they shut off the eastern part of Germany, splitting Berlin into two separate cities. The Russians killed Christians who lived in East Germany whenever they found them. Many Christians hid in tunnels or basements. Some families, whose homes were on the border, would jump out their front or rear windows, depending on the location of the house, to escape living under the Russians.

Anna told me of one young man who smuggled his girl friend out of

East Germany by tying her underneath his car. Fortunately, they made it, but the newspapers featured the story and from then on, the Russians used mirrors to check underneath cars moving out of East Berlin.

Even after the Berlin wall was torn down, Russian soldiers killed any Christians they could find. This should be a warning to us. We need to cherish our freedom, and not let anyone take it from us.

Meanwhile, West Germany thrived. They recuperated quickly from their war damages, The United States helped a great deal in their economic recovery. In East Germany, the Russians did the opposite. They moved many of the large industrial plants out of East Germany and into Russia, providing jobs for Russians, but very seriously damaging the economy in East Germany leaving the East Germans jobless, poor and frustrated.

When the Russians erected the wall in Berlin, dividing the city, they literally divided families. Children who spent the night with grandparents on that night, could not go home. Families who lived across the street from each other or a block or two away, now found they could not visit each other. In some cases, the wall separated husbands and wives. Despite the uproar, there was not anything anyone could do to get the Russians to relent.

Now, Anna could understand the sadness, the lack of laughter. The people of East Berlin were very poor and saw no hope for their future. The Communist Party completely dominated their lives. The Communist party owned all stores. People could not own a business of their own. They could not buy the things they needed or wanted. The government was in control and the people were nothing but tools. The East Germans had finally shaken off the oppression of the Nazi Party, only to now face the same from the Communists. This will always be true when people allow the government to become bigger than the people.

Anna told about going to the meat market with Erika. She asked for seven steaks and the man behind the counter told them they would have to wait. An hour and a half later, they were still waiting. Anna wanted to leave, but Erika said to be patient. When the store was empty, the customers all gone, the man explained to them why he had them wait. He said he knew Erika and her family very well. He would sell them the seven steaks, but he seldom made exceptions because it was too risky because the government had given them strict orders about the distribution of what they had to sell.

The fruit stand opened only once a week. Even then, only one pound of fruit could be purchased per family. The government controlled the people in everything they did, and the people were afraid to open their mouths to criticize because Soviet spies were everywhere. Anna commented, "It was a sad way to live. I didn't have time to think about myself. All I could think of was those poor people who lived in this city that was so beautiful. They spoke the same language I did, and yet, the city seemed as if it were on two different planets, one-half was joy, and the other half fear. The sadness in their eyes told in which part of the city they lived. Songs, joy and laughter were unknown to the people of East Berlin. I was experiencing for the first time, life behind the Iron Curtain."

Klaus was not content just to stay in East Berlin. He spent his time trying to find a way to get his wife, Anna and Birgitta out. A month passed and Anna said she had forgotten how to smile. She thought of her own situation at home and realized that as bad as it was, at times, she wanted to get out of East Berlin and be in her own home. She pledged to herself that if they ever got home, she would do everything possible to make her marriage work. Late each evening she went in the bathroom, knelt down, and prayed to God, asking for His help. And He answered her prayers,

"Pack your bags as fast as you can," Klaus told them as he got Anna and Erika together. "We're leaving at midnight."

Anna could see that Klaus was extremely nervous. They were ready before midnight. Anna felt very sorry for Erika and Klaus as Klaus had a long conversation with his father-in-law. "They hugged goodbye," Anna said. "The old man threw his arms around Klaus, big tears rolling down his face. Erika and her mother were also crying. For everyone it was a heartbreaking good-by. They had no way of knowing if they would ever see each other again.

They parked the car near the Ubahn, where two men met them. One man was tall and distinguished looking, the other short and chubby. The taller one took the keys to the car and drove away. The other one took them for a short ride on the Ubahn which was the subway system under Berlin. Anna had never seen anything like it before and to her it seemed spooky, but her fear kept her from asking any questions. Guards were everywhere they went and their guide showed some kind of ID card each time one of these guards stopped them. Anna said she was afraid to look at the guards.

They went out through a gate and their guide kept hollering at them, "Machen sie schnell! machen sie schnell!" (Hurry up! Hurry up!) They ran down a dark street, until they met the tall man waiting with their car. Anna said she couldn't understand how he had arrived there before they did, but all that concerned her was that they get out of there and get back home.

They got into the car with the two men and drove quite a distance. Anna said no one said a word. She said it was obvious these two men were spies and they all felt it best not to say a word. After a fairly long drive, they stopped again. The men told them to get out of the car. Anna could feel her rapid heart beat. She felt the blood rushing through her head. She was frightened. When she looked up and saw three men standing there with machine guns, she became more frightened. She believed they were going to be killed right there. She started to cry. The short, chubby man told her to calm down. "Just keep very quiet," he urged her. "Everything is going to be okay."

The three men huddled together, whispering. Anna was startled, when what looked like a brick wall, suddenly opened. The only light was the beam of a flashlight held by one of the men. "You must be very quiet," one of the men warned.

It was almost time to feed Birgitta, who was only three and a half months old. Anna was fearful she would wake up and start crying. "What about the baby?" she whispered to Erika. "She's going to wake up soon to eat. She wakes up promptly every morning."

Erika replied, "We will just have to hope for the best."

One of the men told them to take their shoes off. Just past where the wall had turned into a gate was a tunnel. They were now running as fast as they could. Anna was carrying Birgitta, and the exertion caused her feet to burn and her lungs and heart to ache. Finally, Klaus took the baby and carried her for a while so Anna could get some relief. Amazingly, Birgitta slept through the entire ordeal. Anna said that every once in a while, she would hear a peep from the baby, and every time it happened it scared her, for fear Birgitta would start crying and they would be heard. They ran in tunnels for long distances. Then they would come up into a safe house, then enter another tunnel, repeating this several times throughout the night.

It was noon the following day and they were still running through a maze of tunnels, and then on the surface, finally arriving at Checkpoint Charlie, the main passage between the East and the West.

The two men who had led them through all of this had a brief conversation with Klaus and then disappeared. As Anna looked around, she could see the barbed wire dividing the city. Guards with machine guns seemed to be all around them.

People standing at the borders were screaming and crying for mercy, wanting to be with family members on the other side. Suddenly Anna heard gunshots and turned to see what had happened. Two young boys lying in a puddle of blood shocked her senses. "What in the world happened?" she screamed. "Are we all going to die?"

Klaus quickly pulled Erika and Anna away from the gruesome scene. "Calm down," he said. "The worst is over. We have only one more checkpoint to get through."

Anna realized that Birgitta was soaked through and through. She sat down on the curb, changing her and feeding her a bottle of milk. Later she would realize that the baby had gone seventeen hours without food or dry clothes. "Only later did I realize what a miracle God had performed to keep my baby quiet."

Now they had to get in line to get through the last checkpoint. They would have to show their passports and open their suitcases. They stood near the end of the line and soon observed that the policewomen who were doing the checking were not very friendly. Anna noticed that after they had checked suitcases, the women were all taken, one by one, into a private room. She also noticed that as they neared the front of the line that Klaus became very nervous. His face was red and he looked ill. As he looked toward Anna, she was tempted to ask him if he was all right, but she decided to keep quiet.

As she wondered about Klaus, Erika gave her a small push. "You're next, Anna."

This was the moment Birgitta decided to cry. As Anna carried her toward the policewoman, Birgitta cried harder and harder. Anna could not calm her down.

"Open your suitcase," ordered the policewoman.

Surprisingly, the policewoman hardly looked at it, and told her to close it. "Next," she said. So Anna and the baby walked on through and waited outside for Erika and Klaus. "I guess the crying baby had gotten to her," Anna said, "And, I didn't have to go in the room like the other women."

As the four of them walked away from the gate, the two men suddenly appeared with Klaus' Volkswagen. They handed the car keys to Klaus, shook his hand and drove off in another car. Anna, Birgitta, Klaus and Erika drove until the city of Berlin was far behind. They finally stopped, got out, hugged each other, half laughing, and half crying, in relief. Free from the confines of East Germany. Anna said they sat in the grass for a long time, breathing in the clean air of freedom. "We just couldn't get enough of it."

As they sat there, Klaus explained two things that had puzzled Anna. He told them that the two boys who had been shot, were trying to escape East Berlin and had been killed in front of their mother's eyes. The Russians allowed no one to escape, even ten-year-old boys.

Then he explained why he was so nervous. Anna, as the wife of an American soldier, had an American ID card, She had hidden it in her bra, but when Klaus saw them take each women in to the private room, he was afraid they would find that card and wouldn't let Anna through. "I suddenly understood why Klaus' face had turned red. He was terrified for me. I also realized that the baby saved my life by crying. It was another miracle from God."

They were on their way home. Anna said they talked and sang, for the several hours it took to get there.

As they neared home, Klaus finally told the rest of the story. The two men who had helped them had been East German spies. In order to get out of East Berlin, Klaus told them that he was preparing to move back to East Berlin to be with his family. Because of his job, he would be able to bring information from the West that would be valuable to them. He told them he had many contacts with the government.

Anna said, "I'm sure it was very difficult for Klaus and Erika never to be able to return to their home town, but most of all, the worst thing would be to never see their family and friends again. We don't know what happened to Erika's parents, as they never heard a word from them."

Chapter Twelve

Early the next morning they arrived back in Baumholder. Anna went to Erika and Klaus' home first, but as the afternoon passed, she got up the nerve to go check on the apartment. She didn't know what she would find and that made her very nervous. She said, "No matter how uncomfortable the situation was, I really didn't have much choice. I still had a house and husband to care for. Besides, my baby needed her own bed and her own home.

When she got to the apartment she found it empty. All the furniture was gone. She assumed that Jack had moved. In the bedroom, she found her clothes and a few of her personal belongings. She knew what had happened, but she didn't want to believe it. He had promised her he would never sell the furniture again for drinking money, but that's what he did.

The landlady, Mrs. Hahn, lived across the street and Anna went over to see what she knew. She was very happy to see Anna. Mrs. Hahn said, "Through Erika's neighbors we found that you had gone to East Berlin. The newspapers in West Germany were full of news, one big headline after another, and tragedy after tragedy. Stories about people separated from their loved ones, because of the Berlin Wall. Jack is very worried about you, after he found out where you had gone."

Anna didn't know what to say. Everyone in the neighborhood knew of her problems with Jack, that he was the reason she had left. Now she was home and she was glad to be there, even if it meant starting all over again.

For some reason she felt guilty for leaving without telling him where she was going, and blamed herself. She went back to the apartment and called Jack at the base. He was glad to hear from her and promised to be home in thirty minutes.

After she hung up the phone, she became quite nervous, wondering what their reunion would be like. She paced the floor practicing what she would say to him. As he unlocked the door she stood by the window. He walked in carrying a big bouquet of red roses. He had a big smile on his face, his "beautiful white teeth" showing.

"I couldn't help feeling sorry for him as he stood there," she said. "He stood there like a repentant puppy, all six feet, four inches of him. I knew he was afraid I would question him about the furniture, because even the baby's bed was gone."

She said Birgitta didn't seem to mind not having her bed. She had gone to sleep on the floor. Anna had forgotten what she was going to say. In fact, she found herself speechless. Her mind was still full of thoughts about East Berlin, and how the police treated the people more like prisoners than human beings. She felt like she had escaped a very dangerous situation where she might have been shot. Every day there were accounts in the newspapers about people trying to escape. Some made it Many did not. She was glad to be home, Jack seemed glad for her to be back. She said, "For the second time, we started all over again. I thanked God every day for allowing me and my baby to be back in our home in West Germany."

Six months passed as Anna fought desperately to make their marriage work. It probably would have, had it not been for Jack's drinking. Anna said he was a good and gentle man when he was sober, but he just could not stop drinking.

She tried to hide the whiskey and even poured some of it down the drain. That didn't slow him down. He just went out and bought more. The problem was now making a big difference in Anna's life. She became depressed, not caring if she lived or died. She began to question why God had brought her into this world. Twice, she gave up and turned on the gas jets on the stove, but each time, the baby would start crying so hard, she couldn't go through with it. She said it was almost as if the baby sensed what she was doing and in her mind the baby was saying, *Mother, I need you.*

Then another problem surfaced. They were going to leave her homeland. On December 14, 1962, Jack received orders to return to the United States. He had been in Germany for five years. Anna said Jack was very excited. He was ready and anxious to return to the U.S. but Anna was not. She said, "The thought of leaving my home and moving to a country I didn't know, and not knowing the language terrified me."

She told Jack that she wanted to stay in Germany, that he could go home by himself. He became furious. "You're going, no matter what, even if I have to drag you."

He became so upset and angry that it scared Anna. He was determined that she was coming to the United States with him. All of his friends had going away parties for him. One evening when he came home from one of those parties he went to the kitchen, got a knife, grabbed Anna by her hair and held the knife to her throat until she promised to come with him. He threatened, "Under no circumstances will you keep me from going home."

She had experienced many beatings and brutal treatment, but this was a new low. Anna was in shock. She said she was afraid of her husband, afraid to close her eyes at night, afraid to do anything against his will.

The day came when she had to tell her friends goodbye. Erika and Klaus were very sorry to see her leave, about as sorry as she was to go. On her last visit with them they all cried for two hours, just saying goodbye.

She also thought about her family. She hadn't seen her mother or siblings in a long time and wished, desperately, that she could see them. She said, "Every time I thought about home, I felt a knot in my throat that got tighter and tighter."

When they got to the airport in Frankfurt, she pleaded one last time, begging Jack to let her stay. He slapped her so hard that she lost the hearing in her left ear for several weeks.

The other German wives on the same flight seemed happy and anxious. They laughed and were excited. They husbands promised them a land of paradise, a land with no problems and sorrows. Anna felt sorry for them. She was more realistic, knowing that there is both good and bad everywhere, and the good things in life come from hard work.

She did envy them their happiness and wished she could feel that in her life.

Her nose started bleeding as they took off and a kind flight attendant brought her some towels. The lady in the seat behind her took charge of Birgitta.

Army regulations prohibited alcohol on their flights, but someone had smuggled whiskey aboard and several soldiers were soon drunk. Eleven long hours later, the plane landed in Dallas. Jack told her to wait with the baby in the waiting room, that he would be right back. He was drunk and could hardly walk straight. She waited, and waited, and waited. Hours went by, and no Jack. Anna knew very little English, so she could not talk with anyone. It was close to midnight and Birgitta and Anna were both hungry. Anna paced the floor, desperate to hear from Jack.

Many hours later, someone came to her and handed her a phone. Anna answered, but all she could understand was that it was Jack's mother, Mrs. Pearce. They could not communicate and Jack's mother finally hung up. A few minutes later, there was another phone call. This time the woman on the phone spoke German. She told Anna, "I'm a neighbor of the Pearce's. They came and got me because I speak German. I don't know how to tell you this, but Jack is here with his folks in Houston."

Jack was so drunk that he had gotten on the flight to Houston, forgetting all about Anna and Birgitta. His mother knew Anna and the baby were supposed to be with him and that something was wrong, so she called the Dallas airport and had them search for Anna and the baby. They took Anna and the baby to the airport hotel for the night and got them something to eat. After Birgitta had eaten and fallen asleep, Anna stood looking out the hotel window. She saw a group of people out Christmas Caroling and realized that Christmas was less than two weeks away. She remarked, "I felt like the whole world was caving in on me. I was so homesick. I finally cried myself to sleep.

The next morning a young woman picked them up and took them to the airport. Anna did know how to say "Thank you" and that was her reply to any kindness. She said that once she was on the plane she thought a lot about what Jack had done. She knew it was the alcohol that continued to plague their marriage.

They landed at Hobby airport about ten a.m. and Jack was there waiting for them, chagrin written all over his face. She knew he was sorry, but that didn't change how she felt about being left at an airport in a strange country where she did not know how to communicate with the people.

Jack introduced her to his parents, his only brother, Bob, and Bob's wife Pat, and their three children. Jack's parents seemed friendly, but Anna could smell whiskey on their breath the moment they kissed Anna. Anna said she was really not in the mood to meet anyone. All she wanted to do was get on the next plane and head back to Germany. It took only a few days to realize that both of Jack's parents drank heavily. They both worked, but as soon as they walked in the front door after work, they hit the whiskey bottle. By the time dinner was ready, all three of them were inebriated and then they argued constantly. She didn't know enough English to know what they were arguing about, and in a way that made her even more uncomfortable. This went on night after night and Anna hated it. She had no choice, but to sit and listen.

A few days before Christmas, Anna had another new experience. Mrs. Pearce put up her little aluminum Christmas tree, the first one Anna had ever seen. Anna said she gradually got used to it, but it wasn't at all like the Christmas trees she was used to. She started taking Birgitta out for a walk after dark. The neighborhood had a good many decorations, which she enjoyed showing to Birgitta. In Germany, people do not decorate the outside of their homes, and no one puts up their tree until Christmas Eve.

Birgitta loved the lights, and although Anna could not get into the spirit, she tried her best to give this eleven-month-old child a wonderful time. Anna's description of how she felt was unique. "I felt like a tree that was transplanted in the wrong season and was ready to die."

Anna volunteered to cook dinner for Christmas Eve, which delighted Mrs. Pearce. Anna cooked a "good old German dinner." Mom Pearce took out her best china for Anna to set the table. With a stack of dishes in her hand, Anna said, a huge dark bug crawled across her hand and onto the plates. "I was almost hysterical," she said. "I screamed and dropped the whole stack of plates on the floor. I was so embarrassed I just wanted to hide. What a mess I had made, and all that beautiful china was broken into tiny pieces. I had never seen a bug that big. Then I remembered that back home they always said that things were bigger and taller in Texas."

Anna had just experienced her first Texas cockroach. She said that for some time after that whenever she opened a cabinet door, she was scared to death. Her appetite was gone and her efforts to fix dinner seemed wasted. Jack and his parents all drank so much that soon after dinner they were all asleep before Christmas Eve had barely arrived.

At nine p.m. she tired of sitting and watching them sleep, so she dressed Birgitta and they went out to look at all the beautiful decorations. They could see into many of the homes, where families gathered together in the living rooms, laughing and talking, celebrating Christmas Eve. Anna and the baby stood and watched until they felt someone might be coming and then they walked on.

"Softly and with a painful catch in my voice, I sang to myself and to Birgitta, 'Silent Night, Holy Night' as I walked through the dark streets with my little girl. I was wondering what my family in Germany was doing at that moment. I looked up to the sky filled with millions of stars. I asked them to send a message home to let my mother know how much I loved her. I could have walked all night. I was enjoying myself, but the baby grew tired and so we went back to the house."

Everyone at home was sound asleep. No one had missed them. The rest of the Holiday was anticlimactic Jack's vacation had also come to an end.

They moved to Ft. Hood, Texas. Anna had a difficult time acclimating to the hot weather. She said she had to sit in the tub with ice cubes all around her about three times a day, and she still couldn't cool down. Their little duplex did not have air conditioning and the hot nights seemed to be the worst. She found it difficult to sleep. They were sleeping on army cots. Jack's drinking habits didn't improve. The few times he was sober, he seemed to love Anna, but most of the time he was drunk. Then he seemed to hate her with a passion. All he talked about then was the Korean War. At times like that, he acted as if Anna was one of the enemy soldiers. He would beat on her and then the next day, when he saw the bruises, he denied knowing that he had hit her. He would apologize, but the same thing would occur again only too soon.

Anna got depressed again. She didn't care about anything. She inured herself to the drinking, the beatings, his friends. Living from day to day, taking care of the apartment and Birgitta were the only things that kept her going.

One day she got an idea. She had worked for more than ten years in Germany, during which time she had contributed to their Social Security plan. Other German brides told her that once you marry and leave the country, you could ask for the money that had accumulated in your account. She wrote to Germany, requesting her money. Within a few weeks, she received a letter with a check for four thousand marks. This was about equal to one thousand U.S. dollars. But there was a problem. She needed someone in Germany to co-sign the check, exchange it for dollars, and send those back to her. She realized her mother wouldn't help her. She did not even write to Anna, even though Anna had sent her several letters.

She decided to write to Mrs. Damek who had been her boss in Baumholder. They had been good friends and she said she would be happy to help Anna. She asked Anna to write a letter to the courthouse giving her permission to receive the money. Everything was going well. Mrs. Damek wrote back saying that she had the money, but suggested that instead of sending it all at one time, that she would send one hundred dollars a month so that Jack would not find out and take it all from her.

Anna had other plans. She was going to take all the money, buy a one-way ticket home for herself and Birgitta and leave Jack. She sat down and wrote a long letter to Mrs. Damek, explaining why she wanted all the money at once.

She waited for a reply. None came. She waited a little longer. Still no answer. She began to worry and wrote back to the courthouse. In the small town of Baumholder, everyone knew Mrs. Damek and Anna was certain it would be straightened out. Then, she received the bad news. Mrs. Damek, had suffered a sudden heart attack and had passed away. Anna had lost someone she really cared about, but now she was also worried about her thousand dollars. She wrote Mr.Damek, asking him to send her money. He replied he knew nothing about it. There was nothing left to do. Anna had lost her money and her trip back to Germany. She felt that everything was going against her.

Chapter Thirteen

If anything, her situation with Jack worsened. Now that he was back in his own country, he became wilder, and was seldom sober.

Notice how once again, God brought people into Anna's life.

Anna met Bill and Marcy Flowers, their neighbors who lived across the street. Anna said they were quite friendly. Marcy was born and raised in Guam. Bill's family was black. They were both very kind to Anna and she and Marcy became close friends. They were a bright spot in her life. Marcy was determined to teach Anna English. Within six months, Anna was able to carry on a conversation. She mentioned that watching TV also helped a lot in learning English. Marcy watched soap operas with her each day. When Jack fell asleep from his drinking binge in the evening, Marcy would come over and Anna and she played cards until three or four a.m.

Jack became more and more of a tyrant Anna finally had enough. She made up her mind to get a divorce. Marcy went with her to see the lawyer. He asked for a fifty-dollar down payment and this was a problem. Jack gave her no money at all. He bought a few groceries when he was paid and he expected these to last until he bought more. If it hadn't been for Marcy and Bill's kindness in feeding them Birgitta and Anna would have been hungry most of the time.

Marcy said, "If he were my husband he wouldn't have a chance. Every time he comes home drunk and passes out, I would help myself. I would clean out his pockets, take every cent. This way he would be broke and would have to stay sober."

Anna was reluctant. "I have never done anything like that. It would be stealing."

Marcy replied, "You are too goody, goody. You are silly if you don't do it."

Anna returned to the house and Jack was still asleep. She began thinking about what Marcy had said. "In a way, she was right," Anna said. "I looked at his clothes lying there, but I just couldn't do it. No matter what Marcy said and how true it was, I just didn't feel it was right."

In the morning, the lawyer called, reminding her that he needed the fifty-dollar down payment. He said he would not serve Jack with divorce papers until he received it. Anna wanted very much to get a divorce. She finally decided to do as Marcy suggested.

The next time Jack got drunk and fell asleep, she took fifty-dollars. That was all. She was scared Jack would realize what she had done, but he didn't even miss it. This encouraged her and from then on, she helped herself when she needed. She was scared Jack would realize what she was doing, but he did not. She was able to buy a few groceries, but she said it didn't stop Jack's drinking. Nothing did.

When Jack was served with the divorce papers he was shocked. He stopped speaking to Anna, except when he was drunk. Then, he made up for his silence by yelling at her about everything. Verbal abuse and physical abuse were daily events.

Anna decided to get a job. She talked to people at the army base and they hired her to clean Army houses. The pay wasn't great, seven dollars and fifty cents for a three bedroom house, and ten dollars for four bedrooms. They demanded that the houses be spotless when she was through. She had to wash walls and ceilings from top to bottom. Many times it would be late at night before she finished a house. Birgitta went with her, as she could not afford to pay a baby-sitter. She was so tired when she finished, that it was a chore to carry the baby back home.

More bad news soon arrived. The landlord contacted her saying Jack was behind in paying the rent and that they would be evicted if they didn't pay up soon. Anna took all of the housecleaning jobs she could get to try and raise the money. There was one house no one else wanted to clean. It was used for parties and was a tremendous job to clean. The army paid twenty-dollars for the job, so Anna took it on. She worked sixteen straight hours to get it done. When she started home, she was dead tired and said she looked like a chimney sweep. It was well past midnight.

Jack was waiting for her and he shocked her when she found him sober and smiling. She was more shocked when he took her in his arms and held her. She said, "He hadn't done that in a long time. I had almost forgotten what it felt like to be loved. Just a kind word now and then would have meant everything to me. I took a shower and cleaned up. Then Jack told me the good news."

"I got transferred again," he said, "back to Germany for another assignment. I don't have to go, but if you will promise not to leave me, I will go. I love you, Babe. I always have and I always will. I don't know why I act the way I do. I don't want to hurt you or anyone else. You are my life, Anna, and without you I might as well be dead. Please try to remember that no matter what I do, I won't live to be forty-one years old anyway."

When she asked why he had said forty-one, he said he just knew he wouldn't live past that age.

With this plea, and knowing she was going home, Anna weakened. She said that in her heart she knew Jack was a good man. She said he had gone to Korea when he was only sixteen, and that was when he started to drink. She couldn't tell me how he got into the army at age sixteen. All she knows is that he said it was easier to fight in the war when he was under the influence of alcohol and after the war he just couldn't stop.

She added, "I always hoped to be able to change his life. Deep down, I did love him. I knew the real Jack better than he knew himself. So I dropped the divorce papers; Going home was much more important to me."

May 1 1963 they sailed on the Navy ship Ubshure. Jack had a very difficult crossing, unhappy that he had to stay sober for those ten days. No alcohol was allowed. Anna was seasick the entire trip, but she was excited about going home. When they arrived in Bremerhaven, she noticed that the other German brides had relatives waiting for them. As she watched families reunite, she had tears in her eyes, wishing her family had come to meet her, knowing at the same time, that no one knew she was coming.

Manheim on the Rhine River was Jack's new station. He had twenty-four hours to check in so he headed toward the base, and Anna and Birgitta decided to go to Munich and see the family until Jack found an apartment. Anna still missed her mother, even after her mother had treated her so badly. Anna still wanted to see her and she wanted Mother to see her granddaughter.

Munich is twelve hours by train from Bremerhaven and so they didn't arrive until the next morning. Anna became more and more excited as they walked through the streets she had played in as a little girl. She was anxious for Birgitta and grandmother to meet. Things had changed so much with new buildings, shopping centers and new homes that Anna almost became lost. The cornfields near their home were no longer there. The fields where Anna would go after her mother bawled her out, places she could go to be alone, were now the site of a huge apartment complex..

Finally, she spotted the old apartment building. This same building was the one that split in two during the bombings of WW II. You will remember the family lived in a barn for a while, moved into other housing, then back to the barn and finally to a barracks where they lived until the apartment house was renovated. Her mother lived in the building for thirty years.

Anna anxiously rang the doorbell on their second floor apartment. Her mother answered the door and soon as she saw who it was, a look of surprised slipped across her face. Anna wanted to hug her, tell her how much she missed her and get a hug in return. Instead, the look on her mother's face told Anna that her mother was not too happy to see her and she decided the hug had better wait. After they had visited for a few moments, Anna asked if she and Birgitta could stay there until Jack found an apartment, but there was no invitation to come forth. Instead, her mother said, "No American GI's child is going to stay in my home."

Anna prevailed on her to let them stay just the one night, and after some bitter words, her mother finally acquiesced.

"We will leave in the morning," Anna told her. "Then, I won't bother you again."

Needless to say, Anna was once again disappointed, hurt, and upset. She spent most of the night pondering what she had done to her mother that made her act as she did. *Why can't she find any love for me?*

Anna arose early, after a sleepless night. The more she thought about how her mother had always treated her, the angrier she became. Her mother was already up. This time, it was Anna's turn to say unkind things to her mother. They argued and then Anna picked up Birgitta and left.

Anna told me, "All the pain and hurt from the past years and as long as I could remember, turned into bitterness. I promised myself never to see or write Mother again. As far as I was concerned I didn't have a mother." Years later, that would all change.

She bought a one-way ticket to Manheim, where Jack was and boarded the train. She thought to herself, *At least Jack loves me, and the drinking— well, I just will have to put up with it.*

Jack was happy to see Anna and Birgitta. He spent all of the day he had arrived and had already found a one room, small apartment. Anna vowed to herself to be a good wife and a good mother no matter what.

Jack and Anna both liked Manheim, and she was determined to make their marriage work.

Jack was quite gregarious. The problem was that all of his friends liked to drink. As she thought about this, she made a bad decision. Anna decided the only was she could keep Jack happy was to drink with him. Jack liked that. It was easier to get her to drink than it was for him to stop. When Jack had his friends over, Anna would have a drink with them. Her goal was to please Jack. She knew how much she could drink and at the beginning, she knew when to stop. As the days passed, however, she realized she was drinking more and more .When she realized this, it made her very unhappy. She realized that if she continued this way, she would become just like Jack, an alcoholic. She knew what she had to do, and she did it. She quit.

This led to more arguments and discord. Their battles became a daily affair. She had tried it her way and she had tried it his way. She decided his way was more depressing. She did not want to become an alcoholic, so she told him, if he wanted to drink himself to death, to go right ahead, but she had enough. She was not going to drink anymore.

The months had passed by quickly and Christmas time approached. This was always a favorite time for Anna, but this year she was sad and depressed. She said that if it hadn't been for Birgitta, she would not have even put up a tree. But her daughter was three and she was excited that Christmas was almost here. On Christmas Eve, they decorated a beautiful tree and sang Christmas Carols. This cheered Anna. She began to feel like a little girl again. Birgitta's excitement was catching. They finished wrapping some gifts for Jack and as they finished they heard him at the door.

Not surprised, but very disappointed, Anna knew he was drunk the moment she saw him. He could hardly walk as he stumbled through the door. Anna jumped up to try and help him, but she was too late. He fell right into their beautiful Christmas tree. Birgitta was shocked to see her Daddy like this. She ran and hid under the breakfast table. Jack lay amidst the Christmas tree, not knowing what he had done. Anna didn't know whether to console Birgitta, help Jack up, or clean up the mess he had made. The tree and the ornaments were all broken. She had begged Jack earlier not to drink before Christmas Eve and he had assured her that he would not. Anna was so frustrated, she didn't know which way to go. She finally realized that she needed to get out of the house for a while, so she took Birgitta and went to town.

They looked in the department store windows, beautifully decorated for Christmas. The little girl was enthralled with what she saw, and Anna was glad she had taken her away from the mess at home, if just for a little while.

As it grew late, they headed for home and then to bed. It was not at all what Anna had anticipated for their Christmas. She said it didn't seem like Christmas, and she found herself very homesick. Anna said, "The word 'home' sounded so beautiful to me, and yet I had forgotten what it was like to have a real home. It had been eleven years since I had been with my mother and siblings for Christmas. I guess if I had a real marriage and a husband who really cared for me, it would not have been so bad. However, that was only a dream, a dream that always seemed just out of reach."

Anna had enough. Early on Christmas Day, she took Birgitta to the train station, and left for Baumholder, where she had worked previously. She still had contacts there. One couple she knew owned a nice hotel. They hired her to wait tables. They proved to be good people. They provided room and board for Anna and Birgitta. Anna said that she loved the work because she knew many of the people who came to eat and the working conditions were excellent.. "I loved my work. I guess because I knew the people, but most of all, I enjoyed my freedom and peace of mind."

I found out one reason Anna liked the job. It was a customer named Karl. She said, "He was very handsome and we became good friends. I looked forward each evening for the time Karl came in to eat. When he didn't come to eat, I missed him. He was a warm and sincere man. He had a beautiful singing voice. The evenings he came in, we sang duets, which the customers enjoyed. They always asked us to sing more. I loved singing and so did Karl."

Anna took Birgitta with her to work. This was another reason she liked work. With Birgitta right there and everyone so friendly, she felt like those who worked there and many of the customers were family. However, when the evening was over and she and her daughter went up to their tiny room, she felt lonely and depressed. She was glad she had Birgitta. Those bouts of depression led to thoughts of suicide but the thoughts of knowing what that would mean to Birgitta kept her going.

As she and Karl became better acquainted, his attention cheered her up. He was very fond of Birgitta. On Sunday afternoons, the three of them would go for a walk. Between two p.m. and five, the restaurant was not at all busy and Anna was allowed to take off so she could be with her daughter. There was a Sunday in February that was very memorable to

Anna. She said it was a very sunny day with clean, new snow. She said," The snow on the tree branches looked like many tiny little pillows."

As they walked along Birgitta was making snowballs and Anna was picking up fresh snow and eating it. Then she got the first of two surprises that would come about within two days.

As they walked, she told me, "Karl suddenly put his arm around me and said, 'Please marry me, Anna. I will make a princess out of you, and I'll be a good father to Birgitta. Please say yes,' I was so surprised I didn't know what to say. My heart really knew how much I really cared for Karl, but I couldn't tell him that. I need time to think, and besides that I am still a married woman."

Karl seemed to understand and he told her to take her time, that he didn't need an immediate answer.

Anna had so few people that ever told her that they loved her, that she was flattered that Karl really cared for her.

As she went back to work that Sunday evening, she had a hard time concentrating on her work. Her co-workers noticed that her mind was not on her work that evening, as some of them commented to her, that her thoughts seemed to be elsewhere.

"It was like a dream world," she said. "All I could think about was Karl and the wonderful things he said to me. His parents had promised him a house as a wedding present, when he found the right girl."

Karl had told Anna that she was that girl and that he wanted to share his life and his dream with her.

This led, once again, to thoughts of divorce. She decided she would start divorce proceedings right away and then she would tell Karl what she believed he wanted to hear, the word, "Yes." She would tell him how much she loved him, and that she would marry him as soon as she was a free woman.

However, there was another surprise waiting.

Chapter Fourteen

The next day was Anna's day off, and there was a lot to take care of. She was very happy as she thought about yesterday's proposal

She had not been feeling too well, and one of the things she needed to do was have the doctor check her out. She had been quite nervous with all that had gone on. Previously the doctor prescribed medicine to calm her down. She felt that the medicine might be the reason she felt uneasy.

On this day, as she left the doctor's office, she said she said she almost collapsed. She didn't even remember how she had gotten home. Her mind was a blank, until she found herself in their small room at the hotel with the door locked.

The doctor must have made a mistake, she thought. He had told her she was three months pregnant, and that was the second surprise. All she could think of was, *What am I going to do.* Her dreams, her chance for happiness had suddenly disappeared. She cried until she could cry no more. Her thoughts were all about Karl and how wonderful he was to Birgitta and what a good father he would have been.

Now there was to be another baby and the father was Jack, a man she had come to dislike intensely. "The baby was not a baby conceived out of love, but out of duty as a wife."

She called Ingrid, the woman she worked for and told her everything. Ingrid was a close friend. Ingrid advised her to tell Jack. "He's still your husband, and the father of the baby.

Anna wrote a long letter to Karl. She said the paper was soaked with tears. She mailed the letter, packed their things and with Birgitta in hand, she got on a train and returned to Jack in Manheim.

"I knew you would come back home," he told her when she arrived. He seemed pleased that she was pregnant again.

Anna realized there was nothing she could do about it and resigned herself to having Jack's baby. It was very difficult for her to forget about Karl, but she decided to make the best of it.

She had a lot of illness. She had to see the doctor twice a week for Toxemia. He told her she might lose the baby because of this illness. He wanted to put her in the hospital, but she refused.

One evening after she had gone to bed, the doorbell rang. Jack was sound asleep and it took a few moments for Anna get oriented, put on her robe and go downstairs. There was a locked gate outside the garden. Anna had to walk through the garden and unlock the gate to see who was there. As she neared the gate she espied a man on the other side. She didn't recognize who it was until he said, "Hello Anna."

She recognized the voice. It was her brother Hans. She hadn't seen him in many years. Her first thought was that her mother had sent him, and that gave her a moment of joy. But she was wrong. Hans had run away from home and needed a place to stay. Not only that, he had a friend with him. Delight at seeing her brother turned into questions. She found out that the other young man was also a runaway and was down at the corner, waiting for Hans to let him know it was okay.

Not knowing what else to do, Anna said "okay" and she told him to go get his friend.

Anna told me that she hoped that having two houseguests, Jack might slow down with his drinking. Once more her hopes were in vain. She found her brother Hans and his friend enjoyed drinking as much Jack. She found that instead of having one alcoholic to deal with, she now had three.

Hans and his friend evidently enjoyed the hospitality. They stayed several weeks. Anna tried to persuade them to go back home, to no avail. They were getting free room and board, and their alcohol, all at Jack's expense.

Anna had known for a long time that her mother had always made life as easy for Hans as she possibly could. She had spoiled him from the time he was born. He could do no wrong. If Anna and Hans had gotten into mischief together, their mother punished Anna, but not Hans.

As Anna got more desperate to get the freeloaders out of the house, she tried to have a serious talk with Hans, but he just laughed in her face. She finally ordered them to leave. Jack stepped in and told them they could stay as long as they liked. If they were going to continue their stay, she suggested they find jobs. Hans was her brother and she wanted to help him get straightened out. He made it plain that work was not his thing. She was shocked at his attitude and disappointed that her brother was living his life in this way.

Meanwhile her pregnancy reached full term. She started having severe pain, and called the doctor to tell him she was ready to go to the hospital. He didn't think she was ready, and told her to stay at home. She was in pain all night but the doctor was determined he wasn't going to deliver the baby until morning. It was a forty-five minute drive to the hospital in Heidelberg, and Jack finally called a taxi to take them.

When they arrived, the doctor checked her. He said she still wasn't ready and he couldn't understand why she was having so much pain. They administered shots and medication, but nothing seemed to help. For three days she had various doctors see her at the hospital, but none of them could ascertain where the pain came from. When labor finally did start, the pain was very strong. Her skin turned grey. Finally on October 28, 1965 little Jack arrived at ten a.m. He wasn't really little at eleven pounds, two ounces.

Anna said, "After I held my little boy in my arms, I began to cry. I knew I loved him as much as I did my daughter. Now I have a boy and a girl. My attitude changed. I was happy and content, realizing it was not the baby's fault that things did not go well between Jack and me. I was very disappointed in myself, and my marriage to Jack. I was confused and hurt due to the circumstances where I found myself. My pregnancy destroyed my chance for a happy life. The memories of Karl and his love were still beautiful."

Anna's timing for having a baby was all wrong. His birth came just before payday. As a result, Jack only made it to the hospital one time. She knew he would be drunk until the pay was gone. It was the same every month. He spent his pay on drink and then borrowed from anyone who would loan to him enough money for a few groceries and rent. What made it more unbearable, was now her brother and his friend were taking advantage of the situation. Her hopes they might keep Jack from drinking proved futile. Hans obviously had no real concern for his sister. He didn't come one time to the hospital.

There were six beds in the maternity suite and the mothers and babies were in the same room. The hospital expected each mother to care for her own baby. Anna watched each day as visitors came to see the other mothers and their babies, bringing flowers and gifts. It was an army hospital, staffed by military and Anna's limited knowledge of English made it even more difficult. Anna cried because she felt so lonely and unloved. She finally realized that she now had two children who needed a mother's love. She had grown up without a father, and her mother had never shown her any love. As these thoughts passed through her mind, she made a promise to herself. *I am going to do everything in my power to be a good mother to my children.*

She was still in a great deal of pain. That and her family circumstances made her heart feel like she was ready to explode.

So she started praying. She asked God to take the pain away, to give her the strength she needed and to forgive her for the foolish mistakes she had made. In return, she promised to be the best mother she knew how

She said that almost immediately she felt God had performed a miracle in her life. She felt better. Her will to live became much stronger, and she wanted to go home with her baby boy.

The doctors were hesitant to release her because of her pain. She had to have twenty-nine stitches and they felt she needed a lot of bed rest. She insisted on going and they finally relented. She called a taxi and she and the baby returned to Manheim.

She found a lot of difficulty in getting around once she was home, but she managed. Birgitta had been staying with the landlady while Anna was gone and she was glad to see her mother, and Anna was happy to see her little girl.

When Jack and her brother and his friend got home, they were surprised to see her. When she asked Jack for money to buy formula for the baby, he told her he was broke. She had to borrow from the landlady.

Shortly after that Hans and his friend got word that the police were looking for the two moochers, as they were runaway's. Anna still had a difficult time persuading them to leave, but the threat of the police finally motivated them to head back to Munich.

The result was that Anna finally heard from her mother. She sent a letter accusing Anna of throwing her brother out on the street. Anna sat holding the letter for some time, trying to decide what to do. She wanted to write to her mother and tell her exactly what had happened. As she thought about it, she realized it would do no good. Hans was the baby in the family. Their mother not only spoiled him, she felt he could do no wrong. Writing would not solve anything.

Seven months later, Jack's assignment in Germany ended. Anna didn't really want to come back to the United States, but she knew better than to fight with Jack. She said, "As long as I was Jack's wife, my place was with him. The thought of rearing my children in America scared me. I knew this was goodbye to Germany forever."

They took the train from Manheim to Frankfurt. Anna pressed her face against the train window, getting her last glimpse of her homeland. Although she loved Germany, down deep inside her, she felt unwanted. A feeling of desolation and despair washed over her. She still had strong feelings of love for her mother and her siblings and wished that she could see them one more time. Mentally and emotionally, her feelings toward her family were bittersweet. "Yet, one letter from home would have been the medicine to cure my broken heart."

Anna had never felt lonelier than she did on the train that day. Apprehension about the future mixed with leaving her homeland was almost more than she could bear.

Birgitta's excitement over flying on an airplane helped take her mind off her own problems. "Oh, Mommy!" she screamed in delight. "We're all the way up here. Way up in the sky."

Birgitta's excitement could not keep Anna from shedding a few tears.

The plane landed in Chicago around midnight. Anna said she felt like a thief when the Custom's agent started going through their luggage. As they went through Anna's things, the agent pulled out a small plastic bag. He set the bag aside as he closed the suitcase.

Anna questioned why he was leaving that small bag out. She still did not understand much English and she had no way of knowing what he was doing. As she tried to get the bag back, the people in line began laughing.

Anna had planted a small garden in Manheim for tomatoes, radishes and a few other vegetables. When they got ready to leave there, she went out to the garden and pulled some white radishes, the only thing ready to eat. Now the Custom's man said he could not allow her to bring them into the country, which is true of all plants, for fear they will bring in some new disease. There were many German women on the flight. One of them who spoke English tried to explain to the man that Anna wanted her radishes. When he shook his head "NO", Anna realized she was not going to get to keep her radishes. She was quite angry.

"No, he can't have them," she said. They had a stare down for a moment or two. Then, suddenly Anna grabbed the bag out of his hand, opened it and stuffed the radishes in her mouth one after another. Everyone was laughing except the Custom's Agent. He looked baffled for a moment, then shook his head and joined in the laughter. Anna was going to eat her homegrown radishes no matter what.

Anna and the others flew on to Houston, arriving about ten-thirty the next morning. Jack's parents were there to greet them and take them to their home. Jack had four more days of leave, which he spent seeing old friends and getting drunk. He went to Fort Bliss in El Paso and Anna was glad when he finally left to go back to work. She remained in Houston for two months until army quarters were available to the family.

The day Jack left for Fort Bliss, Anna had to go to the hospital. She had a miscarriage. She needed several blood transfusions, and she found new friends. Jack's brother, Bob and his wife Pat, were the opposites of Jack. They were against drinking. Because of that, they seldom visited Anna's in-laws. They came to the hospital and spent a great deal of time with Anna, in case she needed something. Anna found him to be a good man and he and Pat had a wonderful marriage

It would be two months before housing was available and Anna spent that time with Jack's parents. They still hit the bottle as soon as they got home from work and Anna could not decide which was worse, living with them or with Jack. In either case, the circumstances made her miserable.

Anna spent her days in Houston watching television. She kept the house clean and had dinner ready for them when they got home each afternoon. Mom Pearce seemed to appreciate what Anna did to help out, but it was rather a boring time for Anna. She did learn some more English from watching TV, but she said she was bored, lonely and homesick.

She was glad when Jack finally called and told her to come to El Paso. She found living with his parents was as difficult as living with Jack. When they got home, they would pressure her to drink with them. Occasionally she would yield to their pressure, but then she regretted doing it. When she went to bed, she prayed to God to somehow get her out of this mess she was in.

The children and Anna flew to El Paso and got there about the same time their household goods from Germany arrived. The army assigned them to a duplex on the base. They did not have a car, so she spent most of her time with the children on the base. She took daily walks with the m, often walking through the hot, desert like country to get to the Commissary and PX. She did not have much money to spend, so all she could do was look. Jack never gave her any money, so occasionally she resorted to taking money from his wallet, when he passed out from drinking. She used the money to buy the children a little something, or to buy a little food, since Jack never bought anywhere near enough to feed the family.

The situation with Jack continued to worsen. Their next-door neighbor was also a German married to a U.S. soldier. Her name was Inge and for a while, Anna was able to enjoy her company when Inge got home from work. It wasn't long, however, before Inge's husband found out about Jack's drinking problem and the arguments and fights that resulted from that. He told Inge that he did not want her to talk to or associate in any way with Anna and Jack. Anna had enjoyed having someone who could converse with her in German, but now that ended. Anna soon found that although she needed a friend, no one wanted to get involved with them, except for Jack's drinking buddies.

One Sunday, Jack took Anna and the children to visit one of his friends. Jack soon ascertained that this friend did not have any liquor. He quickly got the family and left. They went to another man's house. Anna didn't feel well, but Jack insisted they go. This man's wife was also German and Jack told Anna it would be good for her to have someone she could talk with.

By the time they arrived, Anna was feeling quite ill. She was in a great deal of pain, so much so that she didn't want to go in. She told Jack that she would stay outside with the children. He said he wouldn't stay long. She walked the kids up and down the street for two hours and still Jack didn't show. She was really hurting, so she went and knocked on the door, apologized to Mrs. Donahue, and told her she was going to have to go home.

Here again, we see God at work, bringing people into Anna's life to assist her.

"Perhaps we can get together soon," Mrs. Donahue said. She reached to shake hands with Anna and when she did, she said, "You are burning up. You must have a high fever." She called out to Jack that Anna was sick and that he ought to take her home. He had found that this friend had a bottle and he refused to go. So Anna walked home holding Birgitta by her hand and pushing little Jack in his stroller.

She took four aspirin as soon as they got home, but the pain didn't lessen. She took four more aspirin, but nothing seemed to help. She continued to down the aspirin tablets to no avail. Jack finally came home, upset at her for leaving. She felt too ill to try and explain to him and in his condition, he probably wouldn't have understood.

Anna continued to be in pain for the next two days. By Tuesday, she could barely get out of bed. The pain continued and her head was spinning. She got up to fix Jack's breakfast, and he showed no concern for her condition. He made matters worse by fussing at her because she had not done her usual daily duty of spit shining his boots and his buckle. She even hesitated to mention how bad she felt.

Still taking aspirin, she struggled to take care of her two children. Birgitta was a big help in taking care of the baby. She ran back and forth to bring Anna the things Anna she needed. Anna now felt so bad she could not stand on her feet. To move across the room she had to crawl across the floor.

By bedtime, Anna was very ill. She was scared, because she knew something was terribly wrong. She begged Jack to take her to the doctor, but he refused, saying he had a party to go to, and he took off. Just after she got into bed, she started having chills. Her bed was an old army cot, which was uncomfortable to begin with.

Birgitta was only five years old, but she was much more compassionate than her father was. She made a little bed for herself alongside Anna's cot, so she could help her mother. Little Jack was only nine months old, an age where he needed a lot of attention. Anna felt bad that she was so ill and unable to do all that she should be doing for him, but almost as if he sensed something was wrong, he was quiet and undemanding. He didn't cry, even when it was time to eat. He went for hours past his feeding time and Birgitta took over the feeding duties, along with several other chores. She brought Anna additional blankets and waited on little Jack's and their mother's needs.

At six a.m. Jack stormed in. He was furious. He grabbed Anna by her feet, dragging her out of bed. She tried to get on her feet with what little strength she had. She cried out to Jack to help her. Her vision was impaired. Everything seemed dark, but Jack did not care. He yelled and cursed her because she had not starched and ironed the army uniform he needed for the day.

Birgitta helped her get the ironing board set up and she got the uniform ironed, burning herself in the process, because of vision problems. As soon as she finished she went back to bed.

Jack left for work, still angry, but Anna was accustomed to that.

About ten a.m. she crawled to the bathroom. Her urine was black. Then she really began to worry. She crawled to the couch to lie down and asked Birgitta to go next door to see if the lady was home. "Tell her your mommy needs help."

Anna had never met this neighbor, but she had no other option. Jack had refused to help and she knew of no one else who was at home.

The next-door neighbor, JoAnn, came right away. "I was wondering about you," she said, "because I haven't seen you out for several days."

JoAnn took her temperature. As she removed the thermometer and looked at it, she said, "My god," and ran to the phone. Anna continued to worsen. She was having a hard time being rational. She said she was fighting with everything in her to keep a clear head, but she still found herself talking nonsense. She listened as JoAnn got someone on the phone. "You've got to have a doctor available. They can't all be in Vietnam. If this lady dies, I'll hold you personally responsible."

Then she came back to the couch. She told Anna she had been able to reach Jack's platoon sergeant. He said he would tell Jack to come home and take Anna to the hospital. JoAnn had also made an appointment with the doctor for Anna.

Jack made some stops on the way home and it was obvious that they had been for alcohol. JoAnn was furious. "What kind of a husband are you?" she asked him.

She helped Anna get dressed and then she took the two children to her house, while Jack took Anna to the hospital. The hospital was on a hillside and Jack parked at the bottom of the hill. Anna had to grab hold of cars to enable her to make it up the hill, when Jack refused to help her. She fell several times in the process and fell again in the doctor's office. Jack showed signs of his drinking and so the nurse assumed they had both been drinking and that Anna was drunk. She was very rude and uncaring. Anna sat rocking back and forth in pain. The wait seemed to be forever. She seemed to drift in and out of consciousness. They waited for three hours, when she finally heard her name called. She looked around at Jack, and he was fast asleep in his chair. Anna stood to go in the doctor's office and that was the last thing she remembered.

When she came to, she was lying undressed on a gurney, and two nurses were frantically changing cold towels to try and get her temperature down. "She's so hot the towels are smoking," one of the nurses said to the other.

About that time, a doctor entered Anna's vision. He said to the nurses, "I can't operate until the fever is down." Then he turned to Anna. "Mrs. Pearce I must ask you some questions."

Anna said she realized she was talking German most of the time and she started apologizing, knowing they could not understand. "That's alright," the doctor said. "Just keep talking. It doesn't matter what you say."

She evidently passed out again, and the next thing she remembered was a Catholic Priest, praying by her bedside. She did not remember where she was or what day it was. The priest held both her hands and talked to her for a long time. Then the doctor came back, put his hand on her forehead, checking on her fever. She remembers him as being a very kind, caring man.

He said, "This is the longest working weekend that I have ever experienced as long as I have been in practice, but it was well worth it. You had several kidney stones, one stone as big as a silver dollar. We had to operate, and you are still fighting a high fever. I am puzzled about your husband. We cannot find him anywhere. He hasn't been here at all. No one has asked about you. Don't you have any family or relatives here?"

She told me she was crying as she explained to him, "I am from Germany, but my husband is here."

"Well, we tried to locate him. He took two weeks leave of absence from his company but no one seems to know where he is."

This brought more tears from Anna. She felt abandoned by the whole world. It hurt her very much that Jack didn't care enough to even check on her.

The doctor spent quite a bit of time in the next few hours trying to keep Anna calm to help get her temperature down. He stopped by her bedside often, and talked with her, even though her English was not good. He told her he understood what she was saying. "Try not to get upset," he would tell her. "We will take good care of you here. I will personally make sure of that, but you must promise not to cry anymore. You must have a strong willpower to live. Think about how much your little children need their mother. You still have a long way to go before you get back on your feet."

His talks with Anna motivated her to try to get well. Her temperature went up instead of down and they had to pack her with ice. Nurses worked around the clock changing alcohol towels making every effort to cool her down. She passed out again and finally regained consciousness when her temperature got down to 105 degrees.

At that point she began praying to God to please let her live. She knew she had a responsibility to the children. She realized she was very ill and that her life could end. She felt so bad that in some ways she wanted to die, but her will to live became stronger. She had been in intensive care, for ten days, fighting and crying out to God to spare her life, drifting in and out of consciousness.

On the eleventh day, she finally broke through. The doctor and the head nurse, an Army Captain stood by her bedside. "You made it," they told her in unison. The doctor added, "For a while we thought we had lost you, but now we are sure you're going to make it."

Her fever was back down to 105 degrees and continued to drop slowly back toward normal. They moved Anna from intensive care on the sixteenth day. She said, "It was a miracle. I did not know God the way I know him today. I did not know about His healing power. But He heard my cry anyway, and let me live."

When they moved her into a double room, the other patient was very nice to her. It seemed like everyone in the hospital knew about Anna. Her new roommate told her, "They told me I would have a roommate, but I thought you would never get here."

Anna noticed a beautiful bouquet of flowers by her bedside. She was elated, thinking that Jack had finally come through. The nurse told her to read the card. Then she realized that the nurses on the floor had pitched in and bought them for her. It was an act of kindness that really touched Anna. However, there was still a disappointment that they were not from Jack. "No one had ever done anything like that for me," she said, "and I was almost embarrassed to accept them."

Mrs. Donahue, the woman who was the first to realize Anna was sick, as Anna waited outside her home for Jack, now came to the hospital to see her. She told Anna she had been there several times before, when Anna was unconscious. Because no one from Anna's family came, they had allowed Mrs. Donahue to visit her in intensive care. She had checked on the children regularly and now reported to Anna that her neighbor, JoAnn was taking good care of them, along with her own five children.

Anna was relieved to hear about the children and to know they were in good hands.

Mrs. Donahue came often to check on Anna and to report on the children. Then, one day, she broke the news. "They found Jack, but I don't think you want to know about it. It will only upset you."

"What can be worse than what I have already gone through?" Anna asked. "You might as well tell me. I promise I won't be shocked, and besides I'm going to hear about it anyway."

"Well, he is in Houston, celebrating."

"Celebrating what?"

"Your death, Anna. Fifteen thousand dollars is a lot of insurance money, and I understand he has already spent quite a lot, assuming you are dead."

Anna had promised not to be shocked, but she was. She said she was speechless. The room started spinning, and Anna thought she was losing consciousness again. Mrs. Donahue called for the nurse, who checked on her. "She's fine," the nurse assured her. "Anna is just very weak."

Anna drifted off for a few minutes, and when she was alert again, Mrs. Donahue was still sitting there at her bedside. Anna wasn't sure if she had a bad dream or whether it was reality. The thought that she had married a man who wanted her dead, just so he could collect fifteen thousand dollars of insurance money, petrified her. She had loved Jack, borne his children, given up her home country and family and friends for him. Now he was happy because he thought she was dead.

At this point, her thoughts about being in the United States were mostly negative. She felt she was in a country where she did not belong.

I found it interesting as the story developed how all of that changed. You will see what I mean later in the book.

As she thought about it, she realized God had blessed her with two great children. He had healed her when she was so very ill. God had let her live and that was worth more than anything else. She had a lot for which she could give thanks.

Her health was improving each day. The doctor was pleased with her improvement, and Anna was very glad to be feeling better and to regain some of her strength.

Then, she had another surprise. Jack suddenly appeared. It had been over a month since she had heard from him. He found out Anna was alive and he came to the hospital in a vengeful mood.

Anna said she felt very uneasy when she first saw him. She felt her heart react as he walked in. She said she almost felt guilty to be alive. He stormed in with so much anger that Anna did not even get a chance to say "hello."

"It's all your fault!" He shouted. "It's all your fault."

She said, "He called me the most awful names, names which I can't even repeat."

"So help me," he shouted. "I'm going to kill you."

He raised his fist to hit her, when the nurse, having heard him holler, rushed in.

Anna was shaking and trembling all over. The nurse arrived just in time. Anna had been afraid of Jack for a long time, but she had never seen him this angry before. The hospital called the Military Police and they removed Jack from the premises.

She soon found out that it was not just the loss of the insurance money that angered him. The army demoted him, taking away his stripes and ordering him to Viet Nam.

All of this happening when Anna was still weak, caused her to have a guilt trip, blaming herself for the mess Jack had really brought on himself. *"If I hadn't gotten sick,"* she told herself, *"none of this would have happened."*

She felt sorry that Jack was going to have to go to Viet Nam and fight in another war, but she realized there was nothing she could do about it. She wanted him to understand how sorry she was, but his hate toward her caused him to blame her for all of his problems.

The day came for her release from the hospital. She dreaded to go home. Jack had not shipped out yet, so going home to live under the same roof with him was frightening. She did not know what he might do when he got drunk. Her seven weeks in the hospital had provided a respite from him, but now she would be at his mercy.

She would miss the doctor and nurses who had shown her such kindness. She had tears in her eyes when she said goodbye to them. They had a special place in her heart and her memories.

Chapter Fifteen

If it hadn't been for Anna's children, her life at this point would have been very difficult. The kids were happy to see her when she got home from the hospital. They had missed her, as she had missed them. They were really her only family at this point.

Jack was to leave for Viet Nam in less than two weeks. It was a very tense and stressful two weeks, and Jack did nothing to relieve any of the tension. During the time he would be in Viet Nam, with no other choice, Anna and the two children moved to Houston to stay with the Pearce's. He made the trip with them, but he had nothing to do with Anna. She said the hate showed in his eyes to the point she was scared to look at him. His actions were even worse.

Every night while he was in Houston, he went out and got drunk. To make matters worse, he brought girls home with him, a different girl every night. He would sit and drink with them until late and then send them on their way. Anna said it was obvious he was doing this to punish her, as he would order her to get out of the living room when he brought these women home. Then, there were nights that he didn't come home at all. This even upset his parents, but they sympathized with him having to go to Viet Nam.

Anna said, "I tried to ignore it, I tried to not let it bother me, but seeing him kissing and loving other women when he had a wife and two children was more than I could bear. The pain was too deep to try and explain."

She went with his parents to take him to the airport. He didn't speak to her until just before he left. Then his goodbye was a warning to her that she had better not be around when he got back. "I'm going to kill you for sure," he told her with bitterness. Then he went to get on the plane to Viet Nam.

For several months, Anna and the children lived with the Pearce's. They kept pressuring Anna to drink with them, telling her that it would make things better, but she had seen the results of alcohol and actually resented seeing anyone drink, knowing what it could do to them.

It was one of the blue periods in Anna's life, She felt lonely, and that her life was a big mess. She had no one but God to turn to, and when she was alone the tears flowed freely.

One morning when she went to get the mail, she found a brown envelope addressed to her from Washington, D.C. She opened it and tried to read it, but English was still not her favorite language. When Jack's Dad came home, he read it and explained that the army was sending her an allotment check for $100 each month. She decided to save as much of the money as she could, but Dad Pearce suggested that it might be time for her to find an apartment. Anna felt that they were anxious for her to move on. On New Year's Eve, she and the children moved into their own place. She was very happy to be on her own and to be away from the drinking.

Anna spent much of New Year's Eve night, arranging the apartment and getting the children settled. She met some of her neighbors who all seemed friendly and kind; One of them, Grace, who was the apartment manager became friends with Anna. They drank coffee together in the mornings and Anna baked special German pastries for their enjoyment. Here again, God provides Anna with a friend.

Grace began teaching Anna more English. Anna enjoyed living there with people who were understanding and helpful. Jack never wrote to her and as the months passed, she became worried about what would happen when his year in Viet Nam was over.

As Grace learned of her problems, she advised Anna to get a divorce, even taking her to the lawyer's office. She filed, and on July 19, 1967, Grace took her downtown to the courthouse to finalize the divorce. She was already nervous and in spite of all that Jack had done to her and all of his threats, she was still hurt.

As they sat in the waiting room at the courthouse, she was shocked and surprised when Jack appeared. She said her heart started pounding, and she didn't know what to do. Her lawyer tried to calm her, and then he went over and talked to Jack. Grace translated the discussion between Jack and the lawyer. Much to Anna's surprise, he told the lawyer he wanted to stop the divorce. He told the lawyer he was sorry for everything he had done.

An explosion in Viet Nam injured him and caused him to spend several weeks in the hospital. He said it had given him time to think.

Anna added, "Of course while he was in the hospital, he couldn't drink. Jack said he came all the way from Viet Nam just to stop the divorce, but for me, this was the end. I had tried too many times. Besides, I was afraid of him. I just could not forget some of the things he had done to me, and those chilling threats he had made before he left. I had to go through with the divorce, not just for my sake, but for the children who had gone through so much, especially Birgitta. She too was afraid of her Daddy. She said, "So on this July morning in 1967 I walked out of the courthouse crying. I hardly understood what the judge had said, but it really didn't matter. I felt the whole world was falling in on top of me. I was free of Jack, but not of my responsibilities, my cares, my hurts, my worry. Here I was in a strange county with two children, not knowing where to go or who I could turn to."

Anna was very depressed. She felt desperate. Once again, she started to give up. When she got home, she put the children in bed and turned on the gas jets. She felt that going to sleep would be easy and painless. She pulled up a chair to the table and sat down, resting her head on the table. Anna felt her body relaxing.

Then she heard Birgitta screaming. "Mommy! Mommy!"

Anna said the cry went through her like a shock wave. She ran to the window to get some fresh air. She opened the front door and then ran to check on the children. Birgitta had experienced a bad dream and was sitting up in bed. Little Jack was sound asleep. Birgitta's dream probably saved all three of their lives. Anna picked up both of the children and held them in her arms. She realized what a narrow escape this had been and later would realize that God had once again intervened in her life through Birgitta's dream. "I promised myself to never do that again, no matter what."

You might never guess that Anna has a temper, but she did have one incident, while living in the apartment that got her dander up. Birgitta was in the apartment swimming pool. Anna was walking along the edge of he pool keeping an eye on her. A woman who also resided in the apartments walked past Anna, and then turned back to face her. Anna thought she wanted to exchange pleasantries, so she said "Hello."

"Aren't you the woman from Nazi Germany?" the woman questioned.

Anna replied, "Yes, I am from Germany, but I am not a Nazi."

"All Germans are Nazis," the woman fired back. "And so are you. If I were you, I would take that Nazi kid of yours out of this swimming pool."

It was the wrong thing to say. Anna didn't care that the woman had just come from the beauty shop. She gave her one big push into the swimming pool. "Don't ever call me or my child a Nazi."

Needless to say, the woman whose coiffure was now soaked in chlorine water, was furious, but she never came near Anna again.

Anna decided it was time once again to try to communicate with her mother. She sat down and wrote a long letter. She did not give any of the details of her marriage to Jack. She just told her mother that they were divorced. Anna wanted to go home. Down deep, she hoped her mother would encourage her to come home. She told her mother once again that she loved her. She didn't say anything about coming home as she had neither the money to go, or the courage to ask.

This time, her mother did respond. However, it was not the kind of response Anna had hoped for. There were no words of encouragement, but rather of criticism. Although her mother was not an active Catholic, she did condemn Anna for her divorce and for "bringing shame on the family. You got yourself into this. You need to get yourself out."

It was obvious that her mother was still angry with her, and it seemed that was not going to change.

To make matters worse, Jack was not paying the one-hundred dollars a month for child support that he was supposed to pay. Grace, the landlady, was very unique. She told Anna not to worry about the rent. She also encouraged her to start a daycare for the other working mothers who lived there or nearby.

"Most of these people are working," she said, "and have their children in nurseries. How about you, Anna? You could do childcare. Perhaps they would rather have someone close to home caring for their children, and it would be cheaper."

Anna got excited over the idea. They put together an advertising card, which they posted around the apartment complex. Grace was a big help in letting the new tenants know about Anna, and she soon had more children than she could care for. She charged ten dollars a week per child and was soon able to pay her back rent, buy groceries and she even had money left over. She enjoyed the kids, and her children enjoyed having the others there to play with.

One of the children's fathers was an airline pilot. As he picked up his child one evening, he asked Anna if could stay for a moment to talk with her about an idea.

"You are taking such good care of these children," he said. "They really seem to like you. I am thinking about opening a nursery of my own and I need someone to run it for me. Would you be interested?"

Excitedly, Anna didn't take long to say, "Yes!"

Mr. Washburn, the pilot rented a large house, which provided Anna, not only nursery space, but also a home for her and the children, rent and utility free. She also received a commission of ten percent each week from the revenue. With a home and a job, Anna' problems were pretty well resolved. They made an appointment with the welfare department to obtain a license to operate a public childcare center. The license allowed her to have as many as twenty-two children. She not only enjoyed the work with the children, she also received a side benefit. They taught her English. The kids had as much fun teaching her as Anna did learning and it was a win-win situation. She said, "Together, we had lots of fun and I soon almost forgot the past. I had started a new life for myself. Yesterday was gone, and tomorrow was full of promise."

As the nursery celebrated its first year of doing business, Mr. Washburn became more and more ambitious. He wanted more and more children, but he didn't want to hire any help for Anna. He kept telling Anna she could handle more children, while the Welfare Department was telling him, he needed to hire more people.

Attrition set in as some families moved away, and Mr. Washburn finally just turned the whole thing over to Anna. She settled in with ten children, which she felt she could handle.

One weekend, Anna walked over to the apartment complex to see Grace and to swim in the pool. When she got there, she found a big pool party in progress and Grace encouraged her to stay. She knew if she went home, she would be bored and lonely. Her two children were having a good time at the pool, so she decided to stay.

As the party died down, late in the afternoon, Grace told Anna that her husband was taking her dancing and that they wanted Anna to go with them. Anna found a babysitter, and they drove to Galveston. For the first time in a long time, Anna had some time just to relax and enjoy life. She said she had a wonderful time and that it felt good to laugh again.

Before the evening was over, she met Cookie. Cookie was a Merchant seaman, who lived in Galveston. His proper name was Briscoe Cook. He had just returned from a two-month job on a ship that went to Hawaii.

Anna enjoyed talking with him, but soon forgot him as they headed back to Houston.

A few weeks later, Grace called and invited Anna to come over for coffee. When she arrived, there sat Cookie, waiting to see her.

They started dating and Anna enjoyed going out with him, because it gave her a change of pace, something different to do.

At this point, Cookie quit sailing and went to work as an auto mechanic. This had been his profession before he sailed in the Merchant Marine. Anna soon met his parents, who were both disabled. His father had lost his legs and was confined to a wheelchair and his mother had lost one leg from a Copperhead snakebite when she was only seven-years-old. Anna enjoyed knowing Alice, the mother, because she was German and they could converse in German. Alice paid a lot of attention to Birgitta and Jack and they enjoyed being around her.

In just two months, Cookie had popped the question, but Anna was not ready to marry again. She thought Cookie was foolish to ask so soon. Alice had become much like a mother to her, but she told Cookie, "No." She quit seeing him, but he didn't give up.

Anna started having more health problems. The nursery was hard work, taking care of so many children. It also entailed a big responsibility. She found it more and more difficult to get up in the morning. She didn't feel that it was anything too serious, but she also felt she was not doing her job the way she should, that she was letting everyone, especially her own children, down.

It was her kidneys acting up again and she had to go to the doctor three times a week for treatment. This soon ate up all of her savings, and then she started having problems paying rent and utilities on the house. That was when Cookie called again.

Anna knew she was not in love. Her heart was not in it. She liked Cookie as a friend and she liked his mother, Alice, but she was not ready to make a commitment for marriage. Alice had two sons, but no daughters. She kept telling Anna, she was like the daughter she never had, and it was good to have someone to love. Cookie was determined and Anna was in bad financial straits. She said, "My health went down, and my financial woes went up."

As her health and financial problems worsened, Anna finally decided she didn't have a choice. The only way out was to marry Cookie.

Her logic was not good at this point. She said she had married Jack because she loved him and that didn't work, and now she was marrying a man she didn't love and she hoped things would be different.

If you are single and reading this, understand that kind of logic does not work. Marrying a man who drinks and is an abuser, or marrying a man you don't love, are both bad ideas. Anna soon realized her mistake.

She said the honeymoon lasted about a week. They fought continually. Cookie was extremely jealous and very possessive. He insisted she give up the nursery completely. He also told her she could not communicate with the parents of any of the children she had cared for.

He bought a house on the other side of Houston, to remove her from any of her friends. It was a new home and very nice, and the neighbors were friendly people. However, when Cookie came home from work, if he would see her standing outside talking with any of them, he became furious.

The children were growing up. Birgitta was six and started first grade. Anna still spoke German to the children and she was afraid this would be a handicap at school. The teacher assured her that Birgitta was learning quickly. She was a straight A student. Needless to say, that made Anna proud.

Now watch God at work again.

One afternoon when she came from school, Birgitta asked her mother to attend the PTA meeting the following morning. Anna was hesitant to go because she still did not feel comfortable with her English, but heeding Birgitta's pleas, she attended. She sat for an hour without understanding much of what went on. As she listened, she did hear the accent of the woman who sat next to her. The woman also seemed to have many questions. After the meeting Anna asked her if by chance she was German and she replied, "Yes, and my name is Gunda."

The two women hit it off very well, but Anna was almost afraid to strike up a friendship for fear Cookie would find out and be upset.

Gunda gave Anna her phone number and encouraged her to call. "Maybe we can get together for a cup of coffee."

Anna was anxious to call her. She was excited to find another woman from Germany. Unfortunately, she mislaid the number and it was months later, while doing some cleaning that she found Gunda's number. She immediately called and Gunda invited her over. Anna put away her cleaning supplies, dressed Jack, and paid a visit. She did not have a driver's license, but she knew how to drive a car with automatic transmission. It was a ten-minute drive and they enjoyed the visit.

Gunda shared information about her family. She also had a boy and a girl. The boy was in Birgitta's class. As they visited, there was suddenly a loud knock at the door. When Gunda went to the door, Anna heard a loud voice, demanding. "I would like to speak to my wife.'

"Excuse me. Who are you?" Gunda asked.

Anna had already recognized Cookie's voice. She went to the door to try and calm him, and instantly knew he was very angry. Anna was very embarrassed. She apologized to Gunda, retrieved Jack, and went home.

Cookie got there before she did. She did not understand why he was so angry or why he was home in the middle of the day. She pleaded with him that she had done nothing wrong. That she was just visiting a friend from Germany.

He told her he had called home to check on her. When she didn't answer he came home, saw the car was gone. He knew she did not have a license and probably hadn't gone too far, so he drove around the neighborhood until he found the car.

Anna could not believe anyone could be so distrusting. He was so angry the edges of his mouth had turned white. Then he began to berate her. She said he called her as many vile names as he could call up in his mind. He out-cursed Jack. When he ran out of names to call her, he went and packed his clothes and left. He stayed away for a few weeks, and then returned. She had no idea where he had gone or what he had been doing. She was afraid to ask questions because of his anger. She reflected on the fact that it had been just over a year since she had gotten out of her relationship with Jack, and then because she found herself in a financial bind because of her health, she had jumped into another bad relationship. If possible, this was worse than the first marriage, because on occasion, Jack had shown some love when he was sober. Cookie also liked to drink. He spent his time in nightclubs and bars. When he was home, he found something wrong so that he could argue with her. Anna and the children were scared of him. When his truck rolled in the driveway, their fears came to the fore. He was an extremely jealous man and it just kept getting worse.

While he had been gone, Anna had an opportunity to spend more time with Gunda. She met her husband, Glen, and she realized that this couple had a good marriage. It was the kind of relationship Anna dreamed of, but had never had. They always welcomed her. Anna said, "Never in my life had I ever met anyone as dear as she was and still is. I guess when God picks out a friend for you, he picks only the best."

Christmas time drew near. Anna took the children shopping. The three of them enjoyed all the decorations and the excitement that comes with the season. They arrived home thirty minutes after Cookie expected them and there was another explosion. This time it was the balls off the Christmas tree, thrown against the wall, one by one. At the same time, he was telling the children that there would be no Christmas. The kids were petrified, staring at the now naked tree. Tears came in their eyes and rolled down their faces. Anna became almost hysterical. She told him he was crazy, that he needed to see a doctor. He laughed at her, which was the wrong thing to do.

She was so furious at him. She said, "I picked up the breakfast table, and with almost superhuman strength I threw it at him. He barely made it out the front door."

Later in the evening, he came back and they both calmed down, but they did not speak to each other.

The next morning, Cookie did speak. Because she had defied him, he ordered her to go out and get a job to support her kids.

Her only experience in this country was baby sitting. However, she knew she needed to find something. One of the nearest stores was a Weingarten Grocery. It was a twenty-minute walk, and she decided that maybe she could become a checker. She walked to the store, located the manager and asked for a job. He was very kind to her, and when she told him she had not worked in the United States, he replied that he always needed checkers, especially during the Christmas season and she could start part-time the next day.

When Cookie found they hired her so quickly he was shocked. He admitted he had mainly wanted to scare her, and then he told her he really didn't want her to work. He had pushed the envelope too far and Anna was determined to take the job. She had found a job, and she was going to keep it.

Her second day on the job she was able to handle the cash register by herself. She learned fast, enjoyed the work, and the manager seemed pleased with what she did.

"I wish I could find a few more like you," he told her. He knew how to motivate this woman who had never received much praise. She said, "That really made me feel good. His compliment was like gold."

A few months later, Anna received a phone call on a Saturday afternoon. The woman said, "You don't know me, Anna. I'm Pauline. I am one of your customers and I've been watching you in Weingartens for several weeks, while I was shopping. You always seem to know the prices and all the specials on sale. Would you be interested in working for me doing office work?"

Anna told her she had never worked in an office before. Pauline was very friendly and encouraging. She told Anna that she understood that German people were hard workers. She finished by saying, "If you are willing to learn, I'm willing to teach you. Why don't you come by the Houston House for an interview?"

Anna was interested and excited. Working in an office was like a dream come true. She was anxious for the interview.

When she told Cookie, he immediately objected. A big argument ensued, but on Monday, her next day off, Anna went for the interview. The company was National Car Rental Systems. She recognized Pauline, who was the office manager, as soon as she walked in. Pauline encouraged her as she waited to see Mr. Simmons, the big boss. "Don't be afraid," she told Anna. "Just be yourself."

Anna was still a little frightened when she shook hands with him. He asked many questions. She assured him she would do her best if given the opportunity.

Within a few days, Pauline called and said the job was hers. Anna was elated and quickly gave her two-weeks notice. The Weingarten manager told her, "If you can better yourself, Anna, I'm all for it. I do want you to know you were one of my best checkers and many customers are going to miss you."

On February 13, 1970, Anna started her new job and more than doubled the pay she had been receiving. Pauline was her teacher and Anna said she was very patient with her. One of Anna's greatest fears was using the phone because of her accent, and a natural shyness. However, under Pauline's tutelage she learned quickly. She also had to learn how to type and use the adding machine, but she learned quickly and enjoyed the work very much.

Things at home did not go as well. In fact, Anna said they became more unbearable each day. Cookie did everything in his power to isolate Anna and the children. He sold the house in Houston and purchased a mobile home and two acres of land in New Caney, Northeast of Houston. He left Anna with the job of clearing the brush from the property. Vegetation in this area tends to grow dense and it is not easy work to clear piece of land, but Cookie was very generous. He bought her an axe and a pair of hand clippers and told her to get busy. Anna did just that. She was so proud of the first piece of acreage she had ownership in that she worked diligently.

Cookie gave her more pride of ownership by letting her pay for the land and all the utilities out of her paycheck, while he paid on the mobile home. He also let her buy the groceries. She had nothing left each month for the children or herself, and that was the way he wanted it.

He disliked Gunda very much and was determined to keep Anna and her apart. Gunda was very plainspoken. She didn't hesitate to tell Cookie what a louse and a bum he was. His plan to separate them didn't work.

A few weeks later, Gunda called. "Guess what, Anna. We are moving to Humble. We won't have to call long distance anymore." Humble was just a few miles south and they were back in the same area code. Both women were excited about being able to get together again.

However, Cookie wasn't to be out maneuvered. He forbade Anna to call or visit with Gunda. There was no way he could keep the two friends apart. They called each other while at work every day and quite often visited each other. Anna had to do this without Cookies' knowledge, and that wasn't easy. He refused to let Anna go to Houston, even to buy groceries and he wrote down the mileage on her car and checked it every day to make sure she went no farther than to work. Anna felt bad about deceiving him, and she got away with very little. Then, when he found out she had broken his rules, she paid a price. His abuse was not only verbal, it became physical. She said, "I was in trouble with him, all the time."

One day at work, they got a new shipment of cars. This meant extra work, to get all of the cars licensed and ready to rent out. The manager asked the office help to stay late to get this accomplished. Anna called Cookie to let him know she would be late. When she arrived home, he was sitting in his car and she could see he was angry.

She asked him what was wrong, why he was waiting outside in his car. He answered that he didn't believe she had been at work, and he was just getting ready to come and check on her. The more he talked, the nastier the accusations, and it went downhill from there.

Anna asked again what was wrong. He kept ranting and then he hit her, spit in her face, and locked her out of the house. He refused to let her in. The children were asleep, as he had made them go to bed at five p.m. every day because they were in his way.

Anna went to the window outside the children's bedroom and tapped on the window, but they were sound asleep. The mosquitoes were very bad and Anna had no place to go. Around three a.m., she heard Birgitta get up to go to the bathroom. She got her attention and finally to into the house. She got a little rest in the children's bedroom, but was unable to sleep. Her thoughts were all about Cookie's accusations. In the morning, her allergic reaction to the mosquitoes was very obvious in welts all over her face and arms as she went to work.

The pressure had gotten to her. She could not quit crying, even at work. She trembled and shook all of the time. She began to question what was happening to her. Finally, Pauline asked one of the other girls in the office to take Anna to the doctor. He immediately admitted her to the hospital. He said she was on the verge of a nervous breakdown, and asked a lay psychiatrist to see her. As they talked, Anna began to open up. She told the psychiatrist what was going on in her life. The psychiatrist reassured Anna that there was nothing mentally wrong with her. She gave Anna a sedative, and after two weeks in the hospital, she was able to go back to work.

Cookie continued to make life miserable. He thwarted any plans Anna would come up with to have a little fun or relaxation. Then he went on a campaign to destroy all Anna' mementoes of home. He smashed her watch from Germany. He destroyed all the pictures of her family, and anything else that she had brought from home.

Anna said he went even further. "He destroyed my mind and my faith in people."

She recalled that his mother had told her once, that Cookie hated all women until he met Anna. She felt Anna would get him to settle down, and as things progressed, she was sick and upset that her son was acting in this way. Then Cookie himself started in, telling her that every married woman was no good, because he had had them all, and they were all alike. He said the only way to treat women was like dogs. Anna finally realized that she was married to a very sick and cruel man. She said he enjoyed torturing her and then laughed aloud when she cried.

Anna didn't want to talk about it with me any farther, except to say she was hospitalized three times. She continued to hope he would change, dreading to face another divorce. She blamed herself for two bad marriages. The psychiatrist heard this, and told Anna that it was quite natural for most women to jump out of the frying pan and into the fire, simply because they believed they could not have anything else.

Chapter Sixteen

Here is where I want you to pay close attention. In everyone's life there is a turning point. Sometimes it happens when we are very young. Often it happens as an adult. It can be to the good or to the bad. It all depends on to whom we listen. I am writing these few paragraphs because I would like to see more people aware of the fact that God's Spirit may be using someone to talk to them. Or, His Spirit may want to use you to be the talker, the encourager. Don't miss the opportunity you may be given to help someone come to know Jesus.

God's Holy Spirit tries to work in our lives to lead us toward God. He also uses other people to help point us in the right direction. Oftentimes people don't listen to God's Spirit or to those God sends into their lives to do the Spirit's will. That person may be one of our parents, a relative, a friend, a working acquaintance, or someone you have never met before. The thing is, we need to be better listeners.

A few years ago, I wrote the biography of THE MEANEST MAN IN SAN SABA COUNTY. A working acquaintance and his eight year old daughter were two of the people God's Spirit used to lead Wade Lackey to the Lord..

In Anna's case, it was her friend Gunda. I truly believe God had introduced Anna to others who helped her through some rough spots. Now, God thought it was time for her to meet Him. It would have been very easy for Gunda to choose to stay at home that Sunday evening when Anna and the children came to visit, while Cookie was out on a drinking binge. Gunda was a member of the First Baptist Church in Humble. She had invited Anna to go to church with her before, but Anna, being from a Roman Catholic background, and knowing nothing about Baptists was somewhat reluctant. This evening, she decided to go with Gunda.

"I thoroughly enjoyed it," she said. "It was then when I realized for the first time that there was only one God. For the very first time I saw a Bible up close. I had never been allowed to see a Bible before. Gunda was reading scriptures from it and she showed me things I had never seen or known. The book was so interesting. I could have stayed there all night."

Anna and the children began regular attendance, and in just a few weeks, Anna and Birgitta, who was now nine years old, accepted Jesus in their hearts and were baptized.

"What a beautiful day it was. I'll never forget it," she told me. "From then on, I felt God's presence and guidance more and more."

They joined a small church in New Caney and went whenever Cookie was not at home. He did not allow them to go when he was home. They couldn't even pray when he was there. Anna would tuck the children in at night and then they would pray together. Jack was just four years old, but he liked to pray. "Dear God," he would pray. "Let us be a happy family. I don't want Mommy to cry anymore. Please God, bless us. Amen."

"At times like that," Anna said, "it was hard not to cry. I knew the children were hurting, and so was I."

More and more of the time, Cookie stayed out late, often until three or four a.m. This didn't upset Anna too much. If was a relief for him to not be at home.

Jack, Sr. surprised her with a phone call one afternoon. It had been three years since she had heard from him; He insisted on seeing the children. Cookie didn't like the idea, but he agreed it was better for her to take the children to see Jack than for him to come to their house.

When Anna took the children to see Jack, she was surprised that he was sober and looked good.

"I stopped drinking," he said. "It's been almost six months now since I have had a drink."

You could almost sense what was coming. Anna said it was almost like old times when she had first known him in Germany. He was kind to the children, visiting with them, seeming to enjoy them. Then, when he got ready to leave, he took Anna's hand and said, "Babe, I want you to know I have never stopped loving you. You are the only woman in my life and I want you and the children back. I know you are married, but please think about it. These are my children and we need to be together."

Anna told him she would think about it and she left with the children.

She had been thinking for some time about divorcing Cookie and she knew Jack had a good point. They were Jack's children, and it would be nice to have a happy family. However, there was no guarantee he would not go back to drinking. Her thoughts bounced from one scenario to another. She had good reason to divorce Cookie. Somewhere along the line she had promised God she would not go through divorce again, and the torment of not knowing what to do had her emotions all stirred up again.

That led to thinking about home. She still missed her family and yearned to be able to go back to Germany. Her mother wrote to her occasionally. The letters were brief, just giving a little family news. Anna's siblings were all married and as far as she knew, happily so, and that bothered her that her marriages had not gone well. Anna would go outside after dark and look up at the stars, sending mental messages back home. She would recall the rejection from her mother and some of her sisters and almost persuade herself she had some kind of curse on her. She would end up crying out, "Why me, God? Why me?"

As she became more despondent, she went back to the doctor. He told her she was heading for another breakdown, if she did not get out of her present situation. He warned her, "but this time it won't be at the hospital, it will be in a mental institution." That got her attention.

She renewed her prayer effort. "Dear God, please don't let this happen to me, for my children's sake. Please give me the strength and keep me strong so I can do my job right and concentrate at work, and with my children."

Somehow, God gave her peace about divorcing Cookie. She pretty well made up her mind she would be better off with Jack, now that he was sober and a member of Alcoholic Anonymous. They would start a new life together. She had been impressed with his sober appearance.

I'll bet you can guess what happened.

Two weeks later, she called Jack and suggested they get together for lunch and discuss his suggestion of two weeks previous. Jack showed up and stepped from the car to greet her.

Her greeting was, "Why did you do it?"

Jack was obviously drunk.

"I guess if I can't drink, I might as well be dead."

Words failed Anna. They had a cup of coffee together and Anna went back to work, feeling very hopeless.

As she drove back to work, her heart felt like it was about to burst and her throat ached. She looked up to heaven and once again cried out, "God, hold me while I cry."

She pulled into the parking lot at work and slumped over the steering wheel, crying her heart out. Then God took charge. It felt as if someone put his hand on her shoulder, and then spoke to her. "Anna, don't cry anymore. It had to be this way. You were about to make another mistake."

She dried her eyes, thanked God that the boss and Pauline had both been so understanding, and went back to work. She was more calm and relaxed than she had been in weeks. She realized she had been about to make another big mistake.

When she arrived home, she told Cookie right out that she was through with him and that she was filing for divorce..

He found it amusing, laughing at her. "You will never go through with it. You need me and you don't have a family to go to."

Anna did not know where to turn. Gunda was her best friend, but she had her own family and there was not room for Anna and the children to move in with them. She was afraid to go to sleep at night. She spent her nights in the children's room, but not before Cookie beat and tormented her, even though he promised not to bother her.

One morning on her way to work, she became conscious she was going over the speed limit and was approaching a construction area. She pressed on the brake pedal to slow down, and found she had no brakes at all. Fortunately, she had the composure to use the emergency brake. She finally was able to get the car stopped without hitting anything or anyone. One construction worker stood in front of the car, with no place to go, and was greatly relieved when Anna's car came to a stop right in front of him. Anna said the front of the car was less than a hand's width from the worker. She tried to get out but was so weak, she couldn't move or speak. She said she was sure the man saw the fear in her eyes. She was finally able to tell him she had no brakes. He got in the car and nursed it off the edge of the freeway and to a nearby gas station. Anna felt God's hand in getting the car stopped and then have someone there who would help her.

The mechanic at the gas station checked the brakes and told her someone had tampered with them. His question was, "Who would do a thing like that?"

Anna knew whom. Her mechanic husband. When she confronted him, he commented, "Oh, did the brakes go out?" Then he laughed. Anna said, "I could see his mind was filled with evil."

Pauline directed Anna to an attorney and one week later, he served

Cookie with divorce papers. Cookie was quite surprised that she had gone through with her promise.

She started looking for an apartment, but found the rents were more than she could afford on her paycheck. It was not going to be easy to get away.

With all this going on in her life, she still had to keep her mind on her work. Just a week after her brakes went out, she was coming home from work, driving the speed limit at seventy miles per hour. She heard a strange noise and she believed it was coming from under the hood. The strange part was that when she slowed down, the noise got louder. When she accelerated, it decreased. She got up to eighty-five to stop the noise, and then it happened. The car started sliding from one side of the freeway to the other. Anna was petrified. Telling herself not to panic, Anna was afraid to put her foot on the brake pedal, concerned that the car might flip over. Almost a mile went by as the car continued careening back and forth. Cars behind her slowed down to stay out of the way. Anna was praying and crying, desperate to know what to do. She tapped the brake lightly and the car started spinning, going around and around. She said she heard herself screaming aloud. Finally, the car slid into the grass along the edge of the road and came to a stop.

A truck driver from J.C. Penney stopped to help, but Anna was so frightened, with tears pouring down her face, that she couldn't speak. He asked if she needed a doctor, and she was finally able to tell him "No."

He walked around the car and came back to tell her that both her front wheels were almost off, and that the axle was damaged. He pulled the hubcaps off and discovered the lug nuts were all loose. When he checked the back wheels, he found those lug nuts were also very loose. He said, "Young lady, someone did this on purpose. Have you had the car in a repair shop lately?"

Anna told him her husband was a mechanic and he took care of the car. She knew what had happened. Fortunately, the truck driver was able to tighten the lug nuts and repair the axle. He told her that she needed to check with whoever worked on her car, but Anna already knew. After about two hours of work, she was able to drive on home, this time slowly and cautiously.

Cookie was standing in the driveway when she drove in. He looked surprised to see her. She was furious and ignored him as she went into the house. She was still trembling with fear and his sight made her sick. She also feared for what might happen next.

Later that evening, when she had calmed down, she told him she was going to tell her lawyer about the lug nuts being loosened on her car and what had happened.

Cookie laughed at her. "You don't have proof," he said, "and besides, a wife can't testify against her husband."

Anna said, "He admitted the truth, but was completely calm and cold."

Cookie worked for East Texas Motor Freight and his shift that week was from midnight until six a.m. Anna called Gunda and told her what had happened, and Gunda agreed that Anna and the children needed to get out immediately. As soon as Cookie left for work, Anna packed up their things, and with Gunda, and Gunda's friend, Maryland, they made several trips from New Caney to Humble. By three a.m. they had moved everything. Anna only took personal things of the children and herself. Anna said, "At that time, nothing seemed more important to me than peace of mind. Material things are replaceable, but human beings are not."

The phone calls started coming to Anna at the office. Cookie, telling her she needed to come home. On April 13, 1971, after three years of marriage, she signed the final divorce papers. Cookie already had everything, so he didn't show up.

That afternoon, Anna went back to work, trying to forget the hurt and the pain inside her. She was happy that the children and she were free from this brutal man.

Gunda and her family made room for them, and Anna and the kids enjoyed the time they lived there. They joined the church where Gunda belonged, and Anna joined the church choir. On Saturdays, they went to the mall. About all that they spent was for an ice cream treat, but the children reveled in this time with their mother and no longer had to fear Cookie's violence. Anna said it felt wonderful not to be afraid anymore, or to have to look at her watch every five minutes.

It made a big difference in the children's lives. Birgitta's teacher called and said that for the first time, Birgitta was communicating with the other students.

Anna understood this. She still recalls how shy she had been as a child, because she did not feel accepted by her family. It made her withdrawn and lonely. She hated herself, blaming herself for the fact that she did not feel accepted. She envied the other girls at school, who seemed to always be laughing and having a good time, while her life seemed like drudgery.

She said, "I felt like Cinderella, who wasn't good for anything or anybody, except to dream and do hard work. I knew exactly how Birgitta had felt up to this point."

However, out from under the dominating fear of Cookie, and seeing her mother able to enjoy life again, Birgitta was shedding her shyness to become a well-adjusted young lady.

Chapter Seventeen

I have mentioned before how God has a way of bringing people into our lives, to stand alongside as encouragers when we are going through rough times.

In Anna's case, she had Gunda. Now, Anita, the switchboard operator at National Car Rental also stepped in. She and Anna became good friends. Anna was once again fighting depression and Anita seemed to know what to say, and when to say it. She would invite Anna and the children to dinner, and she often had a word of advice.

"You need to get out of the house, Anna."

"Anna, you will be happy again. Just wait and see. Somewhere out there in this big old world is a man who is just as lonely as you are. Perhaps, he too, had a bad marriage, and if it is God's will, you two will meet. But you must be patient, give yourself time."

Anna knew she was right. She did need to get out, and she had many reasons to be happy. It just took some little reminders.

Anna was not too concerned about marriage again at this point. However, she said, she did do some daydreaming about a man like the one Anita had mentioned. She pictured a tall man, with his hands in his pockets, walking along the street in Houston. Maybe there was a man like that for Anna, somewhere out there

They had been at Gunda's house for several months and Anna knew it was time for her to move on, and find her own place.

A couple at church, the Weisenbakers, had a son who owned a small rental house. It was a little frame house in rather bad shape, but he was willing to rent it for eighty dollars a month, a price Anna could afford. Anna and the children were thrilled to have their own place and they worked at fixing it up. For some time, people had used it just for storage, so there was a lot to do. Anna painted it, inside and out, filled the cracks and holes in the walls. She wallpapered the kitchen. When she was finished she said, "It looked like a castle, our castle."

Cardboard boxes made do as furniture. The big boxes sufficed as tables once Anna put a pretty cloth on them. Summertime was hot, without air conditioning. A lady at work sold her a small electric heater that kept them warm in the winter. A short time later, she established her credit by buying a bedroom suite and a dining room set, and paid them off in six months. Once again, she emphasized to me that material things are not that important. She knew from experience. This was her fourth time to start over.

Anna made up her mind that the following summer she would move back to Germany. She had no reason to stay in the United States. She wrote to her former employer in the flower shop, Mrs. Wagner and told her of her plans. She received a reply from her saying she was happy Anna was coming home. Anna told her she wanted to get back in the florist business. Mrs. Wagner said she was ready to retire and Anna's inheritance would be the flower shop. Anna said, she felt she could have asked Mrs. Wagner for the money to come home, but she wanted to do it on her own. However, saving money was not that easy. Even when she took all the overtime that was available, her expenses ate up most of her income.

Meanwhile, Anita the encourager was still at work. She told Anna about a neighbor of hers, who was recently divorced and living with his parents. His name was Herschel. "You must meet him, Anna. He is a very nice man and who knows, maybe the two of you can get together."

Anna did not feel that she was ready to meet another man. Her thoughts and plans at this point were to get back to Germany the next summer. Anita kept up the PR program, saying Herschel had survived a bad marriage, and that he was the type of man who would really appreciate a good woman.

"Well perhaps someday he will meet one," Anna replied.

However, Anita's campaign was working. Anna started visualizing Herschel as that lonely man, walking the streets in Houston that she kept seeing in her dreams.

A year passed and Anna still had not met Herschel. She thought of him often, although she had not met him.

December came around again. Anna still did not have the money to go home. She promised the children she would take off some time so they could go to the mall and see the Christmas decorations. It was a time of mixed emotions for Anna. In some ways it was her favorite time of the year, but it also brought back memories of home and a loneliness that was hard to deal with. However, the children loved it and she shared in their excitement. Starting December fourth, she took a weeks vacation.

Anita suggested that they go Christmas shopping and have dinner together one day of the vacation. They decided on the day and around eleven a.m., they climbed into Anita's Volkswagen and started out the driveway. Suddenly, Anita excitedly said, "Oh, Anna. There's the man I've been telling you about." Herschel was standing in his front yard. Anita swung into his driveway. "Now, you will have the opportunity to meet my neighbor." Rolling down the window, she introduced her "German friend, Anna. Remember, I told you about her about a year ago."

The hospital had just released Herschel the day before after having gall bladder surgery, and he was still quite weak. He said hello to Anna and the children, told them he was still very weak. After a very short conversation, he went to the house and they left on their shopping trip.

It had not taken much time for Anna to feel a stirring in her heart, but when Anita asked what she thought, her reply was, "Well, I don't know. I just barely met him."

They had a big shopping day, visiting several malls, having the kids pictures taken with Santa Claus, and enjoying a wonderful time together. They returned to Anita's for dinner, and then had a good visit while the children played.

As they visited, Herschel rang the doorbell, returning something he had borrowed from Anita's husband, Ed.

I would suspect Herschel had an ulterior motive.

"Come in," Anita said. "Anna and I were just talking. Why don't you join us?"

In Germany, Anna never wore long pants, only dresses and skirts. She had bought a pair of pants several weeks before this visit but had never worn them. Anita had encouraged her to wear them that day, and now she was embarrassed to have Herschel see her wearing pants.

He didn't seem to notice. He got down on the floor and played with the kids, while Anna and Anita continued their visit. Birgitta and Jack really enjoyed this, as their father and Cookie never seemed to have time for them. It was an instant friendship. Herschel and the kids liked each other. When Herschel left, Anita looked knowingly at Anna and smiled. "Well, Anna?"

Anna blushed and replied, "He seems very nice, but I don't know him."

Evidently, Herschel was impressed. About eight p.m. when Anna and the children backed out of the driveway to go home, he was there to wave goodbye. The kids talked about how nice and how wonderful he was, all the way home. While Anna pondered the feelings inside her, as if she had known Herschel all of her life. The thoughts made her nervous.

She did not sleep well. They had enjoyed a wonderful day with Anita. Then the thoughts of the lonely man she had dreamed of so often crept into her mind. Then she dreamt of home in Germany and her desire to return there. She was determined that nothing would stop her from going home the next summer. She really wanted to return to Germany.

Now, as Christmas neared, Anna found, that as usual, the heartaches and loneliness were back again. She was surprised, a few days before Christmas, when Herschel's mother called her. "Anita says you were a florist in Germany and loved to work with flowers. I wondered if you would be willing to make an arrangement for me. I purchased a beautiful bowl and a candle. I want to make a centerpiece for my table and wondered if you could help me."

Anna was still on her vacation, so the next day she went to the Lybarger's home to help Herschel's mother. She couldn't understand why she was so nervous as she approached their front door, but she was. It was only to help with a flower arrangement, nothing more.

Mrs. Lybarger invited her in and they discussed what kind of an arrangement she desired. Anna picked up the bowl and the candle to take with her and started for the door. Then, Herschel walked in. He said "hello", gave her a warm smile, and invited her to stay and have a cup of coffee with him. His mother was leaving for the beauty shop and Anna could keep him company. Anna was impressed. "How could I say 'no' to a charming man like Herschel? Besides, I was in no hurry, so I accepted his invitation."

It took them three hours to get their fill of coffee, and Anna left, floating on a cloud. "Never in my life, had I met a person that was as easy to talk to as Herschel. He was warm, understanding and very sincere. I could feel the goodness in him. Through the long talk we had, I discovered that he had been deeply hurt in a bad marriage. I couldn't understand why any woman could hurt a man like him, because he seemed to be the kind of man I had always dreamed of. But here I go again, I told myself. I'm dreaming. Inside of me there was a big change. I felt like singing and shouting and all the way home I did sing from the top of my lungs. 'Oh, what a beautiful morning. Oh, what a beautiful day. Oh, what a beautiful morning, Jesus is coming my way.' If anyone had seen me like that they probably would have thought I had lost my senses. But I was happy, and for the first time in many years, I felt the warm sun shining again, deep in my heart."

From those words, I believe we could conclude that Anna was in love.

She was not ready to admit this, however. Her previous experiences made her fearful about showing her feelings. When Herschel would call and ask her out on a date, she had a litany of excuses. Fortunately, Herschel was patient and persistent. Those traits not only helped him in this situation, they impressed Anna.

Finally, she called him and asked him to come for dinner. The children were excited about his coming and that also influenced Anna. Their happiness was very important to her. That dinner broke the ice. Herschel didn't miss a day to either call or come by. Anna said that her life became meaningful again.

Nine months later, on August 12, 1972 they were married. Four times, they asked pastors to marry them and were turned down, because they had been married before. Gunda came through again. She had introduced Anna to a pastor when she first met Anna. When Anna went back to him, he agreed to marry them. Anna had pre-wedding jitters, mainly because of her two previous marriages, but Pastor Phipps came to her dressing room, calmed her down and the wedding was on. His words to her were, "Just have faith, Anna, and everything will be just fine." He prayed with her and minutes later the ceremony began.

Anna wore a long, light blue wedding gown. It was her first time to wear a long gown and she said she felt like a princess. Happiness and fear intermingled in her thoughts. She said she felt God speak to her and tell her, "You will have a real wedding. Today you are to be married for the first time because I am with you."

There had been many times in Anna's life when she felt that she had been forgotten by everyone but God, but He had always been faithful, and she truly felt His presence as she entered into this new relationship. God was with her, and Anna was ready to have a new life.

Many years later, Anna said, "God brought Herschel into my life. He loved my children and me like we were his own. He also helped me to get out of that shell I had been hiding in for so long.

Birgitta and Herschel's niece, Kim, were flower girls and they led Anna down the aisle. Anita, the matchmaker, was her Maid of Honor. Herschel's father had the privilege of escorting Anna.

Anna took a moment to reflect on her own father, and wished he could be there for this occasion. Anna loved her new in-laws and as she walked down the aisle with Richard, they stopped for a moment where Herschel's mother, Ann sat. Hidden behind Anna's bridal bouquet, was a red rose, with a note, "I love you Mom," which she handed to Ann. She wanted her new parents to know that she intended to be a good wife to their son. She thought of her own mother and missed both her parents, but she also loved her in-laws and was happy that they could share in this time.

Jack and Birgitta were happy too. Jack stood by Richard with a satin pillow holding the rings. Anna said she could see the happiness in their faces. They were going to be a complete family.

For the first time, Anna understood English and knew what the preacher was saying and what the vows meant. Anna said, "This was the very first time the wedding vows were meaningful to me, because now I knew what they really meant. Twice before I had said them, but didn't understand any of it. This time it was different. When I looked at Herschel and we began to commit our lives to one another, I knew we both had made a promise from the deepest part of our hearts. More important to me was that I had made a promise to God. I could not believe how beautiful those vows were and how God had translated them to my heart so I was able to understand each word. That made our wedding before God and with God a commitment to one another for life. It was beautiful. In the eyes of God and according to His law, this was, and is my first marriage. I can't begin to tell you how beautiful a marriage can be when God is the center of all things."

The children were almost as happy as Anna. They liked their new dad. Anna thanks God each day for giving them a good dad and her a fine husband, the kind of husband she had always dreamed of.

A few weeks later, on a Sunday afternoon, Anna wrote her mother a long letter. She told her she was married again and that she was very happy. She did not know how her mother would react, and actually there was no reaction for some time. She didn't hear a word. It really bothered Anna that her mother could not share in her happiness. She kept writing, hoping that maybe one of her sisters would respond, but there was no reply. She felt completely abandoned by her family. She wished that she had her dad's address, as she thought he would correspond with her. She had asked her mother to send her his address, but she still heard nothing.

Years later, Anna would find out that when she wrote to her mother and asked for her dad's address, she just heaped coal on the fire as far as her mother was concerned. Her mother had never forgiven Dad for leaving the family. While on this end, Anna became more and more frustrated, not hearing. The pain and rejection from her mother and siblings was still very strong within her. In earlier days, this had caused her to cry herself to sleep on many nights. Now, her happiness in being married to Herschel eased the pain a little. It was almost too good to be true. She was afraid she would wake up some morning and find it had just been a dream. Then, when she opened her eyes and saw Herschel there beside her, she knew it was reality and she thanked God over and over again. He had made the impossible possible. Anna said, "For the very first time after thirty-three years of searching I had found someone who loved me as I loved him."

UPPER: Ten year old Anna at her confirmation
LOWER: Ann with her floral master boss at
20th Century Fox New Years Eve

UPPER:Anna in Bavarian drindl dress
LOWER: Anna with Mrs. Wagner, her first boss

Anna's 200 year old German Bible

UPPER: Catholic church in Munich where Anna attended
LOWER: apartment building built by Hitler where Anna lived as a child

UPPER LEFT: Anna & Herchel's wedding—1972
UPPER RIGHT: Anna & ten month old Birgitta
LOWER: brother Helmut, sister Johanna, Anna,
and her mother at 80ᵗʰ birthday party

UPPER: Anna and friend Gunda
LOWER LEFT: family portrait
LOWER RIGHT: nine year old Herschel, Jr.

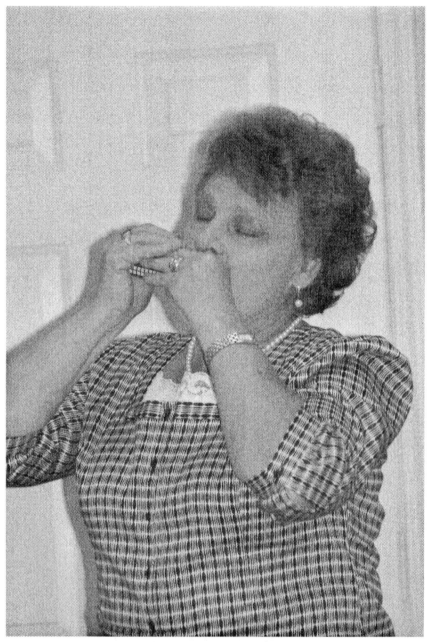

Anna and her harmonica

Anna and her sister Johanna

A scene in Munich today with the bomb shelter Anna and her family used during WWII. The round building in the middle

Chapter Eighteen

Two days after the wedding, Anna was back at work at National Car Rental. She had a new outlook on life. Everything and everyone seemed brighter and sunnier than before. She even enjoyed her work more.

A few months later, a trip to the doctor confirmed that Anna was pregnant. She said the excitement was unbelievable and beautiful. Her love for Herschel made it even more exciting. When she told him, he put his arms around her. She said his eyes were filled with love. They were both extremely happy and they shared the news with the children. The news also thrilled them. The only bad news was that the doctor said it would not be an easy pregnancy and that Anna needed to quit her job, or risk losing the baby. Anna hated to leave the people who had given her such a fine opportunity to start a new career.

It was still touch and go with the pregnancy. Anna had to see the doctor twice a week and each time he warned her not to get her hopes too high. He warned, "I believe you may lose the baby, Anna."

That news worried and depressed Anna. All the way home from the doctor's office she cried and prayed. She really wanted to have this baby. "Please, dear God, don't let me lose this baby."

Her car was an old yellow station wagon. She noticed that when she drove for a few miles, she would get a headache and become nauseated. Twice, she almost passed out and had to pull off the road. Unfortunately, she was having a difficult time with her pregnancy. She blamed her nausea on her pregnancy, and failed to have anyone check the car to see what the problem was.

Going to the grocery store was even a problem. She felt faint and had difficulty breathing. One day she took the kids to the Galleria Shopping

Mall, so they could ice skate. Then they met Herschel for lunch. The children had a good time skating and they stayed so long they got into rush hour traffic on the way home. The traffic was very heavy and as they edged along, Anna once again got a headache and became nauseous. She was glad she had the children there in case she got sick. Then they started complaining about having headaches and feeling nauseous. Anna realized she could smell gasoline fumes and thought she must have a leak in the gas tank. She rolled down her window as they crept along through traffic, but that made her feel even worse. As the children complained more of feeling ill, she encouraged them to sing and talk. Jack said he was tired and wanted to go to sleep. They were stuck in traffic for over an hour. Anna desperately wanted to get off the Freeway and finally was able to get off at the Shepherd Exit. She needed stamps and they were near the post office, so she proceeded in that direction.

As she got out of the car at the Post Office, she looked at the children. Jackie's face had turned pale white. It was obvious that he was deathly ill. Anna could barely stay on her feet, but she knew she had to get Jack home. Before she could move, Jackie went into convulsions and then passed out, his face down on the concrete parking lot, bleeding.

Anna screamed for help and a man coming from the post office, put his jacket under Jackie's head and wiped the boy's face with his handkerchief. As a crowd gathered and Anna spoke about the fumes they smelled in the car, Birgitta also fell unconscious. Anna was crying and feeling helpless. Someone called for an ambulance and the Postmaster, who had come outside, asked Anna for Herschel's phone number. Anna was so upset and sick herself that she couldn't remember his phone number or even the name of his company. An ambulance arrived and administered oxygen to the two children. It took almost thirty minutes for Birgitta to regain consciousness, but Jackie was not responding. All three of them were loaded in the ambulance and rushed to a nearby hospital.

As Anna prayed for God to help Jackie, the medical staff worked on him and in about two and a half hours, he opened his eyes.

Birgitta was able to tell the doctor where her daddy worked and they contacted him. Anna was very happy to see him arrive at the hospital. The doctor told them that the car had a hole in the exhaust system and they suffered from carbon monoxide poisoning. He told them they were lucky to be alive. Later that evening they were able to go home. Anna was worried about the baby she had been carrying, but the doctor said she was fine and didn't need to worry.

However, Anna continued to feel the results of this experience. Several times a day she found herself short of oxygen. She would have difficulty breathing and her heartbeat was rapid. When this happened, the baby kicked constantly, somehow signaling a need. The doctor became worried and that made Anna's anxieties even higher. The baby was due the end of May and on May 1, he said they needed to induce labor. Anna begged him to wait. May 15 is Herschel's birthday and that was the day Anna checked into the hospital. Herschel, Jr. was Anna's birthday gift to her husband on that Tuesday morning in 1973

Anna said he was the ugliest baby she had ever seen. His feet were purple and he was tiny, but she loved him. She said, "He was special to me from the very first moment he came into the world. What a joy it was to hold him, and to know that this tiny, little, innocent bundle was mine. We had come so close to losing him several times, but God had heard my cry and let me keep him. But whenever I held him in my arms, I couldn't help feeling a little strange inside that something wasn't quite right with my baby."

She said he didn't cry like the other babies. His voice was very soft and weak. He didn't eat much. When he was only three days old, he was lifting his head completely off the pillow. The doctors did a thorough examination and pronounced him perfectly healthy. Anna felt better at that point, but there was still a nagging doubt. She did not want to believe there was anything wrong, and yet she felt it down inside her. This caused fear and confusion in her. She was exceedingly happy when they told her she could dress little Herschel, that they were going home. Birgitta and Jack were elated that their new baby brother was coming home. Anna hoped and prayed that little Herschel would grow up to be just like his father.

Two months passed and Anna was still waiting to see the baby smile. When she would talk to him, she got no response. He was old enough to smile or to follow her with his eyes, but he did not. He looked only in one direction and seemed completely unaware of his surroundings. Anna thought it might be a hearing problem, so Herschel and Anna took him to the doctors for a checkup. Once again, the doctor assured them there was absolutely nothing wrong with him and that his hearing was fine.

Baby Herschel got a cold. He cried almost continuously day and night. He broke out in a sweat, and so they returned to the doctor's office and for the third time the doctor told them the baby was all right. Anna knew better. The baby slept very little, ate very little and what he did eat, he vomited back up.

At two and half months, they admitted the baby to the hospital and put him through an extended series of tests. Five days later they got their fourth assurance baby Herschel was all right and they took him home. Things did not improve. He continued crying, ate very little, vomited after he ate and now he was losing weight. When Anna tried to feed him his bottle, he would throw himself backward. He broke out in big beads of sweat, with his head soaking wet.

Another trip to the hospital, this time to check his stomach Again, after a week's stay, tests revealed nothing wrong. He was four months old and had not gained a single pound. Anna and the baby were both staying awake almost twenty-four hours a day. She knew something was wrong, but the doctors could not discern what it was.

Dad Herschel and Anna bought a new home to have more room, now that there were three children. Herschel, Birgitta and Jackie had to make the move, because once again, Anna was taking the baby back to the hospital, this time for a longer stay.. On the seventh day of their stay, as she sat in the hospital room trying to feed the baby, several doctors walked in. One of the younger doctors asked if he could feed the baby and Anna gladly passed the baby to him because every time she tried to feed him, he would arch his back and reject the bottle. She was beginning to think, that after eight years without a baby, she had lost her touch. She almost persuaded herself that she was at fault.

Then, as the young doctor tried to give him the bottle, Herschel reacted the same way. He started to scream and fight as if he were in terrible pain. He threw himself backward and sweat poured down his little body. The doctors immediately all left the room, as if they didn't want Anna to know what they were talking about. A half hour later, they came and took the baby for brain wave tests.

They kept the baby in the hospital and a few days later, Herschel and Anna had an appointment to see the pediatrician at St. Luke's Hospital. As they walked down the hall, they held hands. Anna said their knuckles turned white they gripped each other so hard. When Anna saw the expression on the doctor's face, she knew it was bad news. It was obvious the doctor was having a difficult time telling them. The shocking news was that the baby had brain damage. "The way he reacts, crying, throwing himself backward, breaking out in a sweat tell us he is in pain," the doctor said. "He is having a seizure. During the seizure itself, he probably doesn't feel anything, but he needs to be on medication.

Anna had a hard time getting over the shock. She felt like someone had drugged her. She couldn't speak or move. Herschel had to do the talking.

"How severe is it?" he asked.

"Very severe," the doctor answered. "The central nervous system, the part in the brain that makes everything function in a human body is severely damaged. He will never walk or talk. He will never be able to go to school or play with normal children. I'm so sorry. I have prepared you for the worst. His progress will be very slow."

Anna was finally able to speak. She told me, "Tears were rolling down my face. The room was so very hot, my head was spinning and I was barely able to speak. I felt like I had a rope tied around my throat. Finally I asked, 'Will he look retarded?'"

The doctor replied, "Yes, he will look retarded."

Anna said the words went like a sword through her heart.

Herschel and Anna both left the conference room in tears. Anna said it was the first time she had seen a man cry and she didn't know what to do, how to comfort him. They held each other as they walked back to the nursery. Anna went to the crib and picked up the baby. As she looked at their young baby, she could not stop crying.

The thought kept running through her mind, *Why God? Why this small child? He did nothing to deserve this.* Once again, Anna felt like her life was falling apart.

Anna was exhausted. She was staying at the hospital with the baby. It had been weeks since she had a good night's sleep. For three months the baby had kept her awake every night. The phone in the hospital room kept ringing. Anna didn't answer. She was very tired and really didn't feel like talking with anyone.

Gunda arrived on the scene. Anna said she was like good medicine. Anna cried out her heart to Gunda, who had a way of understanding Anna that no one else seemed to have. She finally persuaded Anna to lie down on a cot next to the baby's crib. Gunda promised to care for the baby while Anna rested.

Anna finally drifted to sleep. When she awoke, Gunda was sitting in a chair rocking the baby and Herschel sat next to Anna. As she looked at him, she began to cry again. He consoled her. She said, "He was not like so many men who cannot cope with situations like this. He was kind and understanding. He put his arm around me and comforted me."

Herschel said, "Honey, we are his parents. We are all that he has. He needs us and we have to be strong. He needs our love and care more than anything else in the world."

Anna told me, "I was amazed at how strong this dear man was. I knew he hurt just as much as I did, but he showed his strength, and that was exactly what I needed. His comfort and concern brought our wedding vows back to reality again. 'For better or worse, for richer or poorer, until death do us part.' How wonderful and secure I felt inside just to know how much Herschel cared for the baby, who was our special child, and for me. We shared the heartache as much as we shared our love for each other. Baby Herschel was our child, no matter what, and that thought brought our family, Birgitta, Jack, Herschel and me, even closer. Each of us drew strength from the others."

A week later, they came home from the hospital. Anna had not even seen the new home that the family moved into the day she took the baby to the hospital. Herschel and the kids had moved everything. Now it was Anna's responsibility to make it a home. It would not be easy. Every time Anna picked up the baby, or even looked in on him, she broke out in tears.

After everyone else had gone to bed that first night home, Anna set about to make their house a home. She said she did not feel tired as she worked all night, putting things away, and hanging things up. She cried some as she went along. She said, "If only I had Mother's or Dad's shoulder to cry on, but I was afraid to write them for fear of more rejection.

By six a.m., she had most of the work done, except for hanging pictures. It was time for Herschel to get ready for work and he was surprised and a little upset that she had worked all night. Anna said she still didn't feel tired. She did not feel like sleeping.

Phenobarbital became a household word at the Lybargers. Baby Herschel had to have two doses of the prescription drug every day to prevent seizures. He did not take kindly to these doses in the morning and evening. He fought to keep from taking it, but Anna persisted, fearing that if she forgot a dose that another seizure would occur. She felt that his life depended on her to administer this to him.

When she went to his crib, there was no sign of recognition. He never smiled. His eyes were glassy, and he stared in one direction. She would hold his tiny fingers, but there was no response. Anna felt that he didn't know her as his mother. He was more like a vegetable. She commented, "The pain in my heart was unbelievable and sometimes I just screamed out, 'Why God?'"

Anna was living like a hermit. After living in their new home for two months, she had never been outside. She stopped communicating with anyone. When the doorbell rang, she didn't go to the door. She spent most of each day sitting by the crib.

She finally brought herself to go out and get the mail. When she opened the mailbox, she found someone had left a book there, titled ANGELS UNAWARE. She realized that someone had come to visit, and when she didn't answer the door, they just left the book.

She opened the book and started reading. She said it was beautiful. She couldn't stop reading until she had read the last page. It helped her to cope with reality. It let her know that she was not alone in her grief and sorrow.

She came to realize that she had to deal with her feelings. Gradually she started going out some. She did the grocery shopping. She covered the baby's face when she went to the store, fearful that someone would look at him and know he was retarded.

The Phenobarbital helped as he did not have seizures as often. When he contracted a cold, he would run a high fever. This would require hospitalization again. When he was two years old, he had the appearance of a six month old.

One of Anna's most difficult times was taking Herschel to the doctor. She would see all the other children running around, talking with their parents and with each other. It almost broke her heart. She said she was hoping and praying that someday her little boy could run, stretch out his arms to her, and call out for his mommy.

When people asked how old he was, she lied to them, telling them, "six months." He was still restless every night, causing her to have many restless nights and never a complete night's sleep.

Her nerves worked on her. One day, while folding the babies' clothes, her whole body began to tremble. She cried uncontrollably. She took some tranquilizers, wanting to get control before Herschel came from work. Nothing seemed to work and before she knew it, she was back in the hospital again, with a nervous breakdown.

At this point, God sent Anna a new friend. Another couple had lived in the house that the Lybargers purchased. They had only been there a few months while they had a new home built. Mary and Jerry Pountain were very kind to the Lybargers. Mary came to visit the day Anna came home from the hospital. Anna said Mary always knew what to say to help Anna feel better. She was very kind and very helpful. Mary was on a mission.

She mentioned the church they went to several times and she had a way of bringing God into the conversation.

When she invited the Lybargers to come to church with them, Anna replied, "We believe in God, but ever since the baby was born with brain damage, I have become rather bitter. She had started going to church again, but she never felt very comfortable. They visited several churches, finally settling on a Baptist Church in their neighborhood. Herschel and the children were going with her. Then the devil stepped in.

It was only the second Sunday they had visited the new church, when the pastor announced that in the evening service, they would have a baby dedication. Baptists do not baptize babies and small children. They believe God wants everyone to make their own decision to follow Him, when they get old enough to understand and make a commitment. A Baby Dedication is more for the parents and the church body to commit to helping raise the child in the ways of God, leading to the child's own commitment and baptism when they are old enough to understand what they are doing.

When the Lybargers got home from church, Anna and Herschel discussed going that evening, to have the baby dedicated, and for them to join the fellowship. Late in the afternoon, a man from the church came to visit, which was not unusual. Prospective members should be visited.

Anna and Herschel told him they were going to come that evening to have the baby dedicated. They were shocked when this man told them that they couldn't have the baby dedicated. That service was just for members.

I don't know if the Lybargers had told him they were going to join, if he didn't hear them, or if he was just plain uncaring. What the Lybargers heard was the fact they couldn't have Herschel dedicated, and those words did a lot of damage. When Anna looked at Dad Herschel, she could see the hurt in his eyes and on his face. It would be several years before that damage would heal.

Chapter Nineteen

The year was 1977. Things didn't get any better. Jack had to have operations on both legs. The Achilles tendons were too short and his feet were beginning to turn inward. Then, Herschel, Sr. had a serious stomach problem and he spent time in the hospital. Meanwhile little Herschel had one seizure after another. The Phenobarbital seemed to have lost its punch. Anna became more and more frustrated. At the same time, she knew that she could not afford another breakdown. Too much depended on her.

She turned to her new friend, Mary Pountain. Mary volunteered to sit with baby Herschel so Anna could get out some.

One day Mary invited Anna to a Bible Study at her church. Anna was not excited about going. She still did not feel comfortable around people she didn't know. At the same time, she did not want to harm her friendship with Mary. Mary was persistent and Anna finally agreed to go. They arrived late and Mary suggested they go through the back door.

As they walked in, Anna could hear singing. There were about twenty-five women standing with their hands raised. Anna thought they must be women preachers and she was in shock. She had never seen many women pastors. Later she realized they were laywomen. They raised their hands heavenward as they prayed. Mary took Herschel to the nursery, where a woman watched over the youngsters. Anna was embarrassed to hold hands with these women she didn't know, but Mary urged her to be a part of the group. Prayer requests were offered up from various group members, but shy Anna didn't say anything.

As the study of the Bible took place, Anna said she did not understand much of what was being said, but she was impressed by women, who seemed like "a roomful of angels," to her.

"I wished that I could be more like them," she said, "I didn't really know how to pray, and besides, I had so many problems." As they prayed for special needs, Anna thought, *If they only knew my needs.*

The longer she sat, the more nervous Anna became. She wanted to escape, to go somewhere and hide. She thought that if she had only brought her own car, she could leave and go home. As they continued to pray, Anna started looking around. She spotted a chair in a secluded corner and headed in that direction with her cup of coffee. Just as she sat, a voice from behind her said, "Hello. I don't think we have met."

So much for being alone. Anna hadn't seen her approach, and it surprised her. "Do you have any needs in your life?" the woman asked. "We'd like to pray for you."

That was all it took to start the tears flowing. As she calmed down, Anna said, "Needs. I don't know where to begin. For one thing, I have a child in the nursery who was born with brain damage."

The woman placed her hands on Anna's shoulders and quickly, other women from the group joined, standing in a circle around Anna with their hands on her. As they were praying, someone suggested she go and bring Herschel to the room. "We will pray for his healing," one of them said.

As Anna approached the nursery, the worker there was praying for Anna and a complete surrender of her life to God. When she returned with the baby to the group, they all laid hands on baby Herschel and prayed for God to heal him.

"I have never experienced a moment more beautiful than that," she said. "I didn't understand all of what was going on, but I felt wonderful inside. I felt like a wilted flower that had just been put into water and suddenly blossomed out."

For a moment, just stop and think of all the people who had an influence for God, a witness if you will, in Anna's life.

Gunda, Anita, Mary, this group of women, and others, all, in some way, had a witness for good to Anna. It is rare when only one person influence a life for Christ. That is why we should never be discouraged when it seems like our witness may be falling on deaf ears. It may take several of God's helpers working with His Holy Spirit, to make a difference.

Anna said on that day, she realized for the first time that when you accepted Jesus into your heart, that from that point on He is always with you and that Jesus has authority over Satan,. She also realized that we can pray to God for healing. That day she committed her life to God and she also committed to do everything in her power to lead baby Herschel,

Birgitta and Jack to Him. She turned over Dad Herschel's illness, their finances, all of our problems to God.

They spent enormous sums on healthcare for the baby. With this commitment, she also realized that God's Holy Spirit, which God puts in each of us, when we commit to Him, was someone she could count on to help her.

In many Catholic churches in the years Anna was maturing, the Holy Spirit was never talked about. Therefore, it was a big change for Anna. She had always sought God's help, but pretty much on her own, and in secret, so no one would laugh at her. When Birgitta and Anna had been baptized years before, the church where they belonged had not taught them as they should have.

Years ago, I wrote a book called NEW BEGINNINGS-HOW TO BECOME A BETTER CHRISTIAN. It had this kind of information in it and in the first church where I introduced the book, the pastor said, "We have members who have been here ten years or more who don't know these things."

Shame on us, as Christians, when we don't do a better job of discipling new Christians. We need to be sure all of the members of our congregation are receiving adequate training.

God had always seemed far away to Anna, and so unreachable. Now she learned that He lives inside us, and that if we give Him the opportunity, He will guide us, love us, and direct us in all that we do.

She said, "What a joy it was to know that Jesus is really there. He knows my heart deep down, and how hungry I was to know Him and His word. He knows the tremendous homesickness I felt for my family and my country. He knows it all. He knew at that point in my life, how hungry I was for my mother's love. As I stood there, soaking wet in my own tears, I felt one last pain like someone was pulling my heart out. I took a deep breath. Mary wiped the tears from my face. I could feel the sweet, sweet spirit of God that covered me so completely. I had goose bumps all over. At that very moment, I knew that God had given me a new heart. All my sins were washed away and I was born again for the second time."

Once again, Anna and her faith would be tested.

She realized that as a new Christian she was like a baby who had to crawl before she could walk. She had a lot of learning to do. For the first time in her life, she opened a Bible and started to read. Some of it did not make sense to her. Going from German to Old English was not easy. She realized she needed to pray about it. She asked God to help her to get the knowledge to understand His word. Slowly, but surely it began to happen, Little by little she began to learn the word of God. As she read, she realized there were some chapters where she would get excited as His word began to make sense to her. The weekly Bible study she attended also helped.

At the same time, things were not well on the home front. Herschel's stomach surgery kept him home and out of work for three months. Without a paycheck, they got in a financial bind. Herschel became depressed. He got quieter and quieter as the days passed. Bills were coming in with no money to pay them. Phone calls from creditors became nastier, and this depressed both of them. The mortgage was three months behind. Anna wished she could go back to work, but realized little Herschel needed her full-time attention. Herschel was still on crutches, but he went back to work.

As soon as he left for work, Anna began her prayer vigil. She was on her knees each morning, pleading to God somehow to open a door for them, before they lost all their material possessions. As she prayed, she felt closer to God. As she concentrated on Him, she felt His presence. She knew she couldn't pay the bills, but she felt a peace in her heart that she had never known before. Now her burdens belonged to God and she was free to have faith and trust in Him.

Read the next paragraph carefully. This was the true turning point in Anna's life.

She said, "The baby seemed to get worse. The seizures came daily, sometimes as many as thirty-five times a day. But I thanked God for giving me little Herschel. For the first time I realized how blessed I was to be his mother and I felt so very honored. God must have thought a lot of me to send this special child to me to take care of here on this earth. I realized that little Herschel belonged to God and I wanted to be the best mother I knew how to be because he needed so much extra love and care. The warmth and security in his home and all around him was the most important part in his life. And I was ready to really give him all of that. I felt God spoke to me and reminded me of all these things. I also remembered how close I came to almost losing him in my fourth month of pregnancy. How I had pleaded with God to please let me keep this baby. I had said I wouldn't even mind if he were crippled or mentally retarded. God reminded of how much the baby meant to me before he was born. So it was up to me to keep my promise. God filled me with love and patience. I sometimes looked in the mirror and asked myself, is it really me?"

Shortly after this, Anna was in her bedroom praying when she heard a loud noise. She jumped up and ran to the baby's room, thinking something might have happened to him. What she saw caused her to scream with joy. Little Herschel had pulled himself up in his crib and stood on his feet for the very first time, something the doctors said would never happen. She grabbed the baby up in her arms. and cried for joy as she held him. What a miracle. Not long after that he began to crawl. Anna worked with him each day to strengthen his legs and to build up his muscles. Almost every day he would pull himself up to his feet, using the furniture. The whole family got so excited, that their screams and laughter scared little Herschel. He was now three years old. The doctors had said he would never stand, sit up or talk.

Although his legs and feet were wobbly, Anna had hope. God had performed a miracle. On that same day as she studied her Bible, she read a passage in Mark 10:27 where Jesus said, "With men, nothing is possible; with God all things are possible if you believe." Anna believed in God and in miracles.

Inevitably, with activity in small youngsters, also come bumps and bruises. One day, Herschel climbed enough to fall out of his crib and when he fell, he cut his tongue quite severely. It was back to the hospital for stitches, which took three hours, and more medical bills. The Lybargers struggled to stay cheerful and happy.

Surprises seem to come in bunches. Shortly after Herschel became very active, Anna had a letter from her sister, Johanna. Anna didn't even finish reading the letter when she ran to the phone. Johanna had included a phone number. She was soon on the line talking with her sister. Anna said that after all those years she sounded different, but she still recognized Johanna's voice. Tears on both ends of the line interrupted the conversation for a few moments, but then they had a good chat. Johanna told Anna that she had been on the waiting list for several years to get a telephone and her name finally got to the top of the list. Anna was thrilled.

Their mother was now living with Johanna, and was anxious to talk with Anna. When Mother came on the line, there was another round of tears. Anna became so excited in hearing from her family, that without thinking, she said, "Momma, I'm coming home."

"Do you really mean that?" her mother questioned.

"Yes, mother."

After that round of excitement and Anna hung up, she came back to reality. She felt that her mother had been excited about talking with her and that she might care, after all, and it would be wonderful to see them.

However, she had told them she was coming home, when she did not even have enough money each month to pay their household bills. Those words she had read in Mark came back to her, that with God, all things are possible. Anna believed what she had read.

Herschel agreed that it would be good for Anna to be able to go home, but he said that financially they just could not afford it.

Then little Herschel got worse. His seizures increased. His tongue had healed, but now bruises covered his whole body from throwing himself around during the seizures. Their doctor took him off Phenobarbital and started him on Dilantin and Mysoline. These drugs did just that. They drugged him, to where he became very inactive again. He didn't crawl and he couldn't stand on his feet Hair started growing on his back. Anna said he began to look like a monkey. This brought more tears from Anna. She wanted to stop the new medications, but was afraid of the seizures. Baby Herschel became very ill. He had colds and allergies, one after the other. He was continuously ill.

One day when Anna gave young Herschel his Dilantin, and Mysoline he fell back and couldn't move a muscle. Anna leaned over him with her ear to his chest and couldn't hear his heart beat. Anna thought he was dead. She ran to call the doctor, who told her to take him immediately to Texas Children's Hospital. It was pouring rain and the streets were flooded as they often are in Houston after a big rain.

Fortunately, Big Herschel was home at the time. Their car was a small Honda, and even busses and trucks stalled out in the high water. "There is no way we can make it," Herschel said. "The car will drown out. Let's call an ambulance."

That did not work either. The ambulances were afraid the high water would keep them from making the run.

Anna kneeled down right where she stood and prayed. "God, he is your child. Please tell us what to do and please save our baby."

Anna sensed that God was urging them to go, so they set out. She said, "The baby is in God's hands. He will guide us and bring us through."

The water came into the car covering their feet, but they made it through. In thirty minutes they had Herschel on a gurney.

The doctor said he was in a coma, and that dehydration would be very harmful if not fatal. He added that if he did come out of the coma, there would probably be more brain damage. Anna said, "I didn't accept that. With my body lying over our baby, I was singing all the songs I had learned in church. I even made up my own words. As I looked at that tiny, little face, I felt like he was only in a deep, deep sleep. Herschel was nervously walking up and down the hallway. I could tell he was filled with grief and pain."

When the doctor checked him again he said he was dehydrating and needed liquid, but that they could only wait and just hope for the best.

As Anna was singing Jesus Loves Me to the baby, he suddenly opened his eyes. Then, to everyone's amazement, the baby stretched out his arms toward his mother and father. They looked at each other and started crying. The doctor brought a glass of water and all he could say was, "It's a miracle. It's a miracle."

There was no more brain damage, and they were able to take him back home that same evening. There was a grateful set of parents that night in Houston, who got on their knees and thanked God for giving them back their baby.

Chapter Twenty

A short time later, Anna was having a restless night. She tossed and turned from one side to the other. When she concluded she was not going to sleep, she began to pray. Something was bothering her and yet, she could not put her finger on it. She almost felt guilty but did not know why. As she prayed, she began to realize she was concerned about big Herschel. He had been very quiet. For several days he had hardly spoken and he seemed very touchy. Something was bothering him.

As she continued to ponder this, she realized it was probably their financial situation. Medical bills had drained their resources. She realized from the things he did say, that he felt bad because he was not able to provide all that they needed. She prayed again that God would help her. By then it was four a.m. The next thing she knew it was seven-thirty and she had slept for the last three and a half hours. More importantly, she felt that God had heard her prayers and that somehow He would answer them.

Around nine a.m. the mailman came. Anna was afraid to even look at the mail. She expected it would be more bills. As she sorted through the mail, she came to a large brown envelope. The return address was the Social Security Administration. Anna was still not fully acclimated to American ways, and her first thought was that the government was going to take the children away from her. She knew of no reason why they should, but somehow the fear came into her mind.

Fearfully she opened the envelope. Inside was a check payable to her for $2,300. She didn't understand and was still not reading a lot of English, so she handed it over to Birgitta who stood nearby.

"Mother, it's a check for $2,300," she said. "The letter says it is payable to you due to the death of Jackie T. Pearce., Birgitta and Jack's father."

There would be a check each month until the children were eighteen. Anna knew nothing about Jack's death. She hurt inside. He was the father of two of her children. He was also the reason she was in the United States. She recalled several years earlier when he had told her he wouldn't live to be forty-one years old. He was forty-one when he died. He had evidently been on disability and this check was a back payment for the months since he had died.

This was a big help in solving their financial problems. They were able to pay off some bills and there was enough money for Anna and Birgitta to go to Germany and keep her promise to her mother.

It had been sixteen years since she had seen her mother and sisters. They planned the trip for June, two months away. Anna had mixed emotions. She was anxious to see her family, but she was also concerned about how they would welcome her. She was finally going to get to go home.

Those two months were not easy for Anna. She started worrying about the plane crashing, how her mother would react, leaving little Herschel, and on and on. She had bad dreams and woke up covered with perspiration. She resorted to searching out scriptures that she could understand. Little by little, God showed her things she needed to know. With two weeks to go, the fear of flying became a big issue. She was fighting a battle with herself about going. One morning as she opened her Bible, she opened to II Timothy. In chapter one, verse seven, it said, "For God hath not given us the spirit of fear, but of power and of love and of a sound mind." That was her answer. She felt God had led her to that scripture, and that she had no reason to be afraid. She had God's promise and He would not break His promise.

She said, "From that moment on, that scripture was my greatest weapon against my fear of the trip to come."

A few days later, they had their bags packed and they were ready to go. Herschel and Jack drove them to the airport. Anna took Baby Herschel to the State Center for The Handicapped so he would get the care he needed while she was away.

Anna said when the plane got above the clouds, they looked like "mountains of snow that hopped from one place to another." She said she felt closer to God. Because of the scripture she had found regarding fear, she had no fear. She was calm and knew that God was with her.

The flight took thirteen hours. A group called the German Liederkranz was on the same plane. These are Germans now living in the United States who gather on a regular basis to sing German songs, and talk about their home country. The women wear dirndl skirts and the men dress in German type clothing. Anna said that on the plane ride, this group kept all the passengers entertained, and she enjoyed singing along with them.

They landed in Frankfurt. Anna thanked God for a safe flight. She said it was unbelievable to actually be back home. They still had a six-hour train ride to Munich, but she was back in Germany.

At four p.m., the train rolled into Munich Haupt Bahnhof (train station). From the train, Anna could see the steeples of the famous Dome called FrauenTurme. This is a large church in Munich. These two steeples were right at 100 meters tall. She had walked up there when she was a lonely teenager.

Birgitta noticed the tears in her mother's eyes as they stepped from the train. It was probably difficult for her to understand the emotions running through Anna as she was back home for the first time in sixteen years. Anna was happy as they walked into the station. Her tears were tears of joy. There is no place like home.

She called her sister from the station to tell them they were in Munich. Her sister and her mother now lived in Peissenberg, which was still an hour's train ride. As they got off the train with their suitcases, Anna looked for her sister, realizing that she might not recognize her after 22 years. She had not had an opportunity to see Johanna on her trip 16 years before because Johanna had moved away.

As Birgitta and Anna started into the terminal, Anna kept searching for someone she knew. Then, about 200 yards in front of her, a woman stood with a big bouquet of flowers. Anna dropped her suitcases and started running and her sister, Johanna, ran toward her. There was lots of hugging and some tears as they held each other.

Anna was still nervous about seeing her mother. She said her heart was pounding as they walked up the steps to the second floor apartment. When the door opened, her mother stood there with her hand outstretched to shake Anna's hand. That was not going to do it for Anna. She threw her arms around her mother and pulled her close. It was the first time in her life that Anna could remember holding her mother like that. Anna said, "Tears were running down our faces. What a precious moment it was, especially for me."

The next few days were special for Anna. Her mother, of course, had aged, and I imagine her mother saw a lot of maturity in Anna since she had seen her last, sixteen years before. Anna said it seemed almost like a dream. She had to keep questioning herself as to whether this was real.

Each night she knelt down and thanked God for this opportunity to see her mother and her sister again, and just to be home.

"My dream was reality, and I was home," Anna commented. "Mother and I were reunited, but this time Jesus was with me, and I knew I had His blessing. My visit home was beautiful."

The only thing that hurt was the fact that her sister Waltraud would not talk with her. Anna attempted to talk with her on the phone, with no success. She didn't know if Waltraud was upset that Anna had married an American or if it was that she had left Germany. It hurt Anna and she knew her sister needed her prayers. The rest of the family was upset that Waltraud acted this way, but none of them had the answer as to why. Anna felt that this visit was an opportunity to witness to her family about God's love. The family was surprised at the change in Anna.

She said, "I wasn't the same Anna I used to be. I was a new creature. I was born again. For me, there was no reason to be angry. I loved my sister and now even more, for I loved her with the love of Jesus. I knew God would take care of it. When the time is right, my sister will forgive me, for my life belongs to God now, and everything in it."

The days rushed by faster than Anna would have liked. There was not time to do all that she would like to have done. She enjoyed being able for her family to know Birgitta. She showed her the school she had gone to and where she used to play, and where she hid when she was lonely. She said the memories were like a book she had just opened. Some of them were happy, but most of them were sad.

An argument arose over Anna seeing her dad. Her mother would not tell her where he was, and did not want her to go see him. "But I have to see him, Mother," she insisted. "I won't go back to the United States without seeing Dad. I know he hurt you deeply, but he is still my father."

Anna found out where he lived from an old school friend. Her mother finally calmed down and agreed that it was all right for her to go. Anna felt that deep down, her mother still loved him. Anna called him and he was excited about seeing her.

He had not changed much from the last time she saw him. He was healthy and distinguished looking for his age. He took Anna and Birgitta out to eat. They visited the botanical gardens where Anna had studied for her Master Gardener degree years before. At the end of the day, it was hard to say goodbye. Anna said it had been a glorious day. Now it was painful to say goodbye. Her dad held her close and kissed her. "He held me in his arms as I had never been held before —so much love. Tears were rolling down his face. 'I will call you as soon as I get back to the United States,' I promised. It was the hardest goodbye I have ever experienced."

Their stay lasted for a month. Anna said it was probably a long time for Birgitta, but it was too short for her. With just a few days remaining, she devoted the time to her mother. They went for long walks together. They reminisced, which brought both tears and laughter.

As they came to the last two days, Anna noticed a change in her mother. She was sad, and went to bed early. Anna went to her mother's room to check on her, and found her crying. She didn't want Anna to leave. Anna promised to come back in two years. She sat with her mother until three a.m. She told her about God, and what He had done for her. How He had changed Anna's life.

Her mother got out of bed and told Anna to come to the cellar with her. In the basement, her mother went through an old hope chest until she found what she was looking for. She handed Anna a large book that had a cover over it. As Anna opened it, she found it was a German Bible. It was Anna's first time to see a German Bible. She said she didn't know that a German Bible existed. Her mother gave it to her along with a black metal cross that was also in the chest. For years, it had hung on their kitchen wall.

"Take good care of it," her mother said. "You are the fourth generation that has had possession of this Bible. I know you love God, and I want you to have it. I know it is in good hands. God bless you, my child."

Anna was elated. She not only had a German Bible that she had longed for, but her mother showed her love for Anna. She said, "Now I had the Family Bible which was more than 200 years old in my hands. What an honor it was for me to receive it. For the first time, I knew and was sure, that my mother loved me."

Birgitta and Anna prepared to fly back to Houston. The night before they were to leave, Anna had a terrible dream about the plane crashing. She sensed that Satan was trying to attack her faith, and that wasn't going to happen. At the airport, Birgitta and Anna went to the chapel, knelt down and prayed thanking God for the time they had spent with her family and asking for a safe journey. As she stepped on the plane, she felt the fear leave her. God gave her peace.

Her mind was full of sweet memories as they winged their way back to the United States. It was a bittersweet time for Anna. She had enjoyed being back in her childhood home, seeing her family again. Sixteen years was a long time to be away. However, she was also anxious to get back to the two Herschels and Jack. On the flight home, she thanked God again and again that she was able to make the trip. She thought about her dad, and how wonderful seeing him had been. She remembered her promise to him to call him as soon as she got home.

However, it was a promise she would not be able to keep,

Chapter Twenty-One

Herschel picked them up at the airport and they had a happy reunion. He was glad to have the family back together again, and Birgitta and Anna were glad to be there. Jack and young Herschel were also pleased to have their mother and sister back home.

They had only been home for a little while when Anna received a telegram. Her father had passed away very suddenly. It was a real shock, but Anna was happy she had gone to see him. Birgitta and she were the only members of the family to have seen him in many years. Anna had always thought her mother would go first, because she had aged so much and had been ill, but instead it was her dad. Up until this trip she had never even had a picture of him, but the pictures she took the day they were together came out well, and are now priceless memories.

The children were already looking forward to the start of school just five weeks away. Anna got busy on the sewing machine getting clothes ready for Birgitta and Jack. While discussing school with a neighbor, this woman told Anna that her little girl went to a special school because of a learning disability. "You ought to register little Herschel," she said. "They have classes for retarded children, and the earlier they start the better.

Anna had not been aware that such classes existed. She called for an appointment with the school administration office. Mrs. Simon, the woman in the administration office was friendly and helpful. The bad news was that there was a long list for children wanting to enter the learning disability program. She told Anna some of them had been waiting two to three years for admission. "It will be almost impossible to get Herschel into school this year," she told Anna. However, she promised to do her best.

Herschel was three years old at the time. He still did not walk. He never reached out for Anna or his dad, but when Mrs. Simon leaned toward him and smiled, Herschel reached out toward her and then put his arms around her. His actions moved both Anna and Mrs. Simon. "None of these children have ever loved me like that, or put their arms around me," Mrs. Simon said as she wiped away the tears.

Anna knew by some of the things she said, that Mrs. Simon was a Christian. Her parting words were, "I'll do all I can to get Herschel into school this year, but it is still in God's hands, and really humanly impossible."

Herschel was now crawling and could hold himself up on his elbows. His parents looked at each achievement as a miracle, and a big improvement for their little boy.

Two weeks after Anna had met with Mrs. Simon, she received a call saying they would not be able to admit him into school that fall because of the long waiting list.

Anna was depressed when she first received this word, but consoled herself with the realization that it was all in God's hands. The start of school was still one week away. Anna felt God was telling her that he would go to school and on faith, she went out and bought him school clothes.

Two days before school was to start, Mrs. Simon called back. "Mrs. Lybarger, I don't know what happened, but Herschel's name is at the top of the list. He will begin school in two days. Isn't that a miracle?"

The news moved Anna to tears. It was a miracle, but somehow she already knew it was going to happen. "I just wanted to give God a great big hug for loving us so much."

Anna missed having Herschel at home. She waited anxiously each day for the school bus to bring him home. Her anxiety lessened, when after about two weeks, she realized that Herschel really enjoyed going to school. Mrs. Monzingo was his teacher and she worked patiently with him day after day, treating him as if he was her own child. Herschel responded affectionately to her loving care. This relieved Anna's fears.

Having known some of these teachers for the handicapped in the past, I have to add that they are God's special people. Everyone I have known in this field loved God as well as the children they worked with.

Herschel's progress was very slow, but there was progress and Anna was very thankful for that. The doctors had prescribed many medications for him. These kept him rather doped up, but they hadn't stopped the seizures. Anna said their medicine cabinet wouldn't hold all the medicine he had to take. Some nights Anna would wake up and go to his crib, lay her hands on him and pray in Jesus' name that he would be healed.

"Oh, dear God," she prayed. "Tell me what to do. He is all yours. Does he need all that medication? Why am I so afraid to stop the medication when I know in my heart that it is poison for him, and as long as he is taking it, he will never get any better?"

What happened next is not explainable. When we put all our trust in God, things happen that are beyond our reasoning.

Evidently, subconsciously, Anna quit giving Herschel his Dilantin and Mysoline. She didn't really intend to stop, for fear the seizures would get worse or something else would happen. She woke up around three a.m. one morning and realized she hadn't been giving him his medication. She had made a practice of marking on the calendar each day when she gave them to him. When she looked at the calendar, it had been almost two months that he had gone without them. Surprisingly, during that time he had not had any seizures, and was sleeping better than he ever had.

She said, "God had completely erased the thought out of my mind and made me forget the medication. What a miracle. I felt like singing and shouting in the middle of the night. God is so good. His love and mighty power are so real and almost impossible for the human mind to comprehend."

At this point they started giving young Herschel vitamins, rather than the prescription drugs. Later in the year, the school called and wanted to know what had happened to little Herschel. Suddenly, he was responding to everything. He started to walk. The family and the school were both ecstatic. Anna said this was a great opportunity to share the miracles of Jesus with others.

The next year Herschel continued to do very well. He had not had a cold or an allergy attack. He was walking better and his little legs grew stronger each day. Everyone at school loved him because he was always happy and cheerful. It was a great thrill for his parents to see him walk to the school bus instead of someone carrying him.

Two years slipped by. Anna was once again on her way to Germany to visit her family. Herschel insisted she go, telling her she needed a vacation. He knew how much she wanted to see her family and to visit in Germany.

She said as she sat on the airplane and looked out at the beautiful clouds, her thoughts were on God, and all the miracles He performed in her life. She was especially thankful that little Herschel had not had a cold, or a seizure in two years. He was walking now, and quite healthy. His brain damage would not improve, but he was well, strong and happy. She felt it was a great testimony to share with her family about what God had done.

She no longer had a fear of flying. God's peace was overflowing in her for one of the few times in her life.

She said, "What a joy it is to know Jesus, to have a deep love for Him and to feel close to Him. My life without God would be empty and meaningless. I don't believe I could have coped with all that had happened in my life without Him. He put the broken pieces together and made something beautiful out of my life. I am a new creature and I am proud of it."

Once again the plane landed in Frankfurt and she took the train to Munich. Her mother was pleased to see her and it was wonderful to be home. All of the family worked to make her stay pleasant. Anna was even able to locate and visit an old school friend, Elfreide, after 28 years of being apart. It was a wonderful reunion between the two friends.

She went to the cemetery to visit her dad's grave, remembering the great visit they had two years previous, just before his passing. She put flowers on the grave and sat quietly reminiscing until it was almost dark. She mourned his loss.

She had neglected to call her sister Waltraud, remembering that on her last visit, Waltraud had refused to talk with her and Anna didn't know what to say or do. After she had been there several days, Waltraud called their mother. She did not know Anna was there. Their mother told her of Anna's presence, and then called Anna to the phone. "Your sister wants to speak to you."

Anna was pleasantly surprised. Her heart beat faster as she answered the phone. A little later as she hung up, she had tears of happiness in her eyes. Waltraud wanted to see her. "Tomorrow I am going to spend the day with my sister," she told her mother.

Anna had been praying daily since her last visit about her relationship with Waltraud. She said she knew that God would open the door when the time was right. Her mother was skeptical, remembering how badly Waltraud had treated Anna two years previous,

Anna told her mother, "Waltraud is my sister and I love her. I am looking forward to seeing her. I have waited too long for this precious moment. Twenty-two years is a long time."

She found her sister looking well. She lived in a beautiful home. They talked together over a cup of coffee and Anna told her sister about Jesus and what He meant in her life. She told her that she couldn't have survived without Him.

Waltraud was disinterested and changed the subject. Anna was not discouraged. She had planted a seed with God's help. She would continue to pray that God's Spirit would nourish that seed and change Waltraud's life.

They talked about other things for several hours and then Anna had to leave. It was difficult to say goodbye. Anna felt that Waltraud still did not understand how much Anna loved her and that the hours they spent together were precious. As Anna walked to the bus stop, they waved to each other once more. It had been a wonderful time for Anna that she had longed for over an extended period of time. She cried as she rode the bus back to her mother's apartment. She struggled with her emotions wondering why she loved her family so much, a love not returned in kind. She contented herself with the fact that she had enjoyed two opportunities to see them after so many years of absence.

She was reluctant to leave, but she was anxious to get home to her family in the U.S. Herschel and the children were at the airport to meet her, and she received a "wonderful welcome." When little Herschel saw her in the terminal, he started laughing. He ran to her and stretched out his tiny arms. He threw his arms around her neck and kissed her over and over. He really surprised her when he said, "I love you." It wasn't very clear, but to a mother who had been waiting for five years to hear it, it was music in her ears. She said, "I looked at him and I saw the most precious gift that anyone could have. I just couldn't stop thanking God for all the miracles He had performed. My baby son was and is, truly God's special person, and He gave him to me. I never felt more honored than at that very moment. Life is good."

Chapter Twenty-Two

Fast forward to 1980. Birgitta is now a young lady, having graduated from High School. Jack is just starting High School. Both children make their parents proud as straight A students. Once again, Anna felt blessed by God that they both did so well in school.

Herschel reached his seventh birthday and was still going without medication. This was his third year without medication and without sickness. Talking has come slowly, but he does say a few words. He knows Jesus and when they would sit down to eat, he would bow his head and want to pray.

Anna said that when she mentioned the word Jesus, Herschel's little arms would fly up in the air, praising Jesus. She said, "He is truly a gift from heaven."

Christmas has always been a favorite time of the year for Anna, and now she is able to decorate their home and yard like those she had admired when she first came to the United States, and then enjoyed when the children were small, as they toured the neighborhood.

"Now," she said, "we were in a position to decorate our home and yard, and I hope other people's children enjoy seeing our decorations"

The whole family participated. She said it was a special time. She still suffered moments of depression, missing home and her family in Germany. She still dreamed of being in Germany for the holidays. Then the mood would change and she would find herself baking cookies and stollen, (a Christmas bread,) making candy, and singing Christmas Carols.

December 4 was one of her favorite days. That was the anniversary of when she met Herschel. It is a day of celebration for the couple. They exchange small gifts, nothing extravagant, but gifts from the heart. Anna loves to cook, so she prepares a special dinner and they eat by candlelight. They had been married nine years at this point and Anna said, it was still very romantic. The children were included and they all sat around the table after eating. On this anniversary, she noticed that husband Herschel and the kids all had big smiles on their faces as they finished dinner. Then, together, they handed her an envelope. "Merry Christmas, Mother," Birgitta and Jack said in unison. "We decided to give you your Christmas present early." Big Herschel sat quietly and smiled.

What a surprise. As she opened the envelope, she pulled out an airline ticker from Houston to Munich. She said she screamed, then cried. She could not believe it. Her dream of being in Germany for Christmas once more, was to become a reality.

The thought of leaving her husband and children at Christmas interrupted her joy for a moment. They quickly reassured her. "Don't worry about us. We will manage just fine. We can sacrifice one Christmas without you. You have sacrificed so many without your family. Besides, we have Dad's side of the family here."

With just one week to pack and get ready, Anna did it in two days. She was so excited and thankful that she had such a wonderful and understanding husband and family.

On Sunday morning, December 14, 1980, she stepped from the plane in Munich, Germany. It had been years since she had seen snow in the wintertime. Houston is not known for its ski runs. The beauty of the glistening snow dazzled her senses. The wooden fences were covered with pillows of snow, as were the branches of the beautiful Blue Spruce and the Tannen Baume, (fir tree).

Anna said you could smell Christmas in the air as she stood in the terminal waiting for the bus to take her into the city. She took one deep breath after another, as she asked herself, *Is it really true that I am spending Christmas in my own country?*

She was enjoying the moment so much that time pretty much stood still. She had not told her mother she was coming. She wanted to surprise her. She had written Mrs. Wagner and told her. Her luggage had been lost, so as she waited for the airline to find it, she spent the day with Mrs. Wagner, recalling old times. They walked into the downtown area to see the Christkindel Market. There were gifts there from all over the world. Around five p.m. it turned dark and when that happened, the whole city lit up like one big Christmas tree. Trees along the street glistened with tiny lights and the town tree had over ten thousand lights, a sight, Anna says she will never forget.

About ten p.m., Anna's luggage finally arrived. On Monday she took the train to Peissenberg. What a surprise for her mother and her sister Johanna. As she walked through the downstairs entry, she hesitated. She wasn't quite sure what to do as no one knew she was coming. She brought a small artificial tree with her, and now she decorated it with candles. She was about ready to climb the stairs and make her grand entry when she heard someone coming. She set the tree down beside her, not wanting a stranger to think she was silly.

As she looked up the stairway, here came her sister Johanna and Johanna's husband, Hans. They came right past her, said "Hello," and started on out, passing right by her as she looked at them.

Suddenly, Hans turned around. He ran back to Anna, and hugged her, while Johanna stood there wondering what was going on. Who was this strange woman that her husband was hugging. As Anna looked at her, recognition finally dawned, "I can't believe what I am seeing," Johanna cried out.

Then the three of them lit the candles on the little tree and walked upstairs. Their mother opened the door, surprised that Hans and Johanna were back so soon.

"We brought you an early present," Johanna said, as Anna peeked between the branches of her little tree. Then she could stand it no longer. "Hello Mother," she said. "Merry Christmas."

Mama was shocked into silence. Tears filled her eyes. She looked at Anna and asked, "Are you really going to stay for Christmas?"

"Yes Mother, and for New Years too."

They both wiped away the tears, and with her arm around her mother, Anna walked into the living room. Hans and Johanna left to do their Christmas shopping while Anna and her mother sipped tea and brought each other up to date.

The next few days were full of present wrapping, singing Carols, listening to favorite Christmas music and reminiscing. Anna said she and Johanna were as small children again, filled with the awe and excitement of Christmas. One evening as they sat listening to music, Johanna put her arm around Anna and said, "I know what you are thinking. I have thought about it every Christmas from the time you left home. But this will be a good Christmas, better than all the ones in the past. Not only for you, but also for mother." Anna added, "And she was right. Johanna has a special place in my heart."

Christmas Eve day came quickly and Johanna woke Anna yelling, "I have a surprise for you." Anna opened the curtains to a beautiful snowstorm. It had snowed all night. Three feet of snow covered the ground, more than Anna would see in Houston in a lifetime. There was a small balcony and Anna stepped out there where she could see the neighborhood children sleigh riding and building snow castles. Others were shoveling to clear the walkways in front of their houses.

Anna thought about her children in Houston who had never seen snow like this. Then, she thought of her own childhood, and how lonely she had felt at times. Quickly, she ate breakfast and got dressed. Soon she was outside shoveling snow and enjoying the winter weather.

Her mother was concerned that she was spending time out in the cold weather that she was not used to, but Anna said it was very exciting. She told her mother, "I don't get to do this sort of thing everyday. Besides, the fresh air is good for my lungs and my complexion."

As the afternoon progressed, everything seemed to quiet down. The stores all closed at two p.m. so people could be at home decorating their trees and finishing other preparations for Christmas.

Johanna, Hans and Anna decorated a beautiful Blue Spruce tree Hans brought home. Hans told Anna he had bought it especially for her and that it was the prettiest tree in town.

Anna and Johanna were like two small children, laughing, singing and dancing around the tree. They soon had their mother laughing with them. Anna said they were the happiest sisters in town and their mother joined in their happiness.

The moment finally came they had been waiting for. Traditionally, they had always waited for midnight. As the clock struck twelve, they lit the candles on the tree and turned out the lights. Anna was thrilled. She peeked outside, "where everything was dark except for the whiteness of the snow," she said, "the big flakes dancing in the air. What a beautiful Christmas. The music was playing and we all stood around the tree singing, 'Silent Night, Holy Night.'

"For me, this was indeed a very special night. As I looked at the sparkling tree, it seemed like each flame of the burning candles had a special message for me. I knew in my heart how much my family loved me and how much I loved them. Quietly, I moved my lips thanking Jesus for making my dream come true. Deep inside I wanted to shout it out loud. I took a glimpse toward mother. She was standing beside me and I saw tears rolling down her small face. I reached out for her, and at the same time she reached out for me. We cried in each other's arms. Mother was trying to say something, but she cried so hard she couldn't talk. Gently, I smoothed my hand over her soft gray hair. 'No need for words, Mother,' I said, 'I love you and I know you love me. This is a new beginning for both of us.'"

Her mother finally was able to stop weeping and dry her eyes. As she held Anna close, she said, "I just can't thank your husband and your children enough for sending you home."

It had taken many, many years, but Anna and her mother were at last at peace with each other. God has a way of mending relationships if we just keep praying and trusting in Him. It is not a time to harbor grudges, but a time for prayer and compassion.

Anna forgot the days of disappointment in her childhood, when her siblings received much nicer gifts than she did, or when her mother had given her to another couple. She was thrilled that her husband and children had been thoughtful enough to purchase the airline ticket for her so that she and her mother could realize how much they loved each other.

She said, "It was much more than a plane ticket. I received healing in my heart. The scars disappeared. I felt like someone lifted me up so high that I could almost reach the stars. I knew it was the love of God. I felt closer to Him than ever before. Oh, how much He loves me – more than I will ever deserve.

"The days seemed to pass faster and faster. New Year's Eve was here. Together, as a family with all my brothers and sisters, we toasted in the New Year of 1981. The church bells all over the city were ringing, bringing in the New Year."

It was a precious moment for Anna. She praised God for His blessings, and for her family, in Germany, and in the United States.

Chapter Twenty-Three

Anna, Herschel, and the children lived in Spring, Texas until 1985. At that point, Herschel's job with Otis Elevators called for a transfer to Beaumont, Texas.

Young Herschel, whom the doctors had said, would never walk, had now become very active. He became very nervous and hyperactive. Anna says that she blamed this on the move. New surroundings, a change in homes, friends, and activities seemed to upset him very much.

One night, Anna tucked him into bed about nine p.m.. She stayed up to hear the ten o'clock news. Herschel Senior had been called out on an emergency service call. He was always on twenty-four hour call. Around eleven p.m., Anna heard the doorbell ring. She knew Senior had a key, and she wondered who would be ringing the doorbell that late in the evening. She was a little anxious and apprehensive, so she called out, "Who is it?"

The answer came in a very soft voice, "Me."

When she got to the door, it was little Herschel. She thought he was asleep, but he had raised the window, climbed out, evidently fallen over the top of a window flower box to reach the ground. Anna said he must have become scared of the dark and soon found his way around to the front door. Anna spent the rest of the night sleeping in his room to keep watch and the next day, they had to screw the window in his bedroom down to shut off his escape route.

Herschel continued to find a way out and run away. Anna became very concerned about his welfare. He did not speak well enough to tell anyone where he lived.

A short time later, he disappeared again while he was supposed to be napping. Anna found the back door ajar. She had to drive around the entire neighborhood searching for him. She finally found him, walking with his teddy bear, several blocks away.

Perhaps the most interesting experience was the day Anna was working in her flowerbeds. She heard sirens coming from all directions and they all seemed to come to a halt right at the Lybarger front door. An ambulance, fire trucks and police cars were all in the Lybarger front yard. As firemen and police descended on the house, Anna thought they would break the door down, before she could get to them. She kept asking what the problem was, and they kept telling her they had an emergency call from that address. "It is not here," Anna told them. But they kept insisting. Anna was stymied. Finally, the ambulance driver told her, "Someone from this house called 911 and when the operator responded, whoever was on the line was making noises that sounded like mumbling or groaning. We thought someone was badly hurt or having a heart attack. It sounded quite serious because the caller couldn't talk. He was only mumbling."

Anna immediately knew where to look. She found little Herschel with the phone. Then she realized he had seen something on TV where someone called 911. He tried it out. His mental state was supposed to be that of a three-year-old, but in some ways he seemed much more developed.

It wasn't long before he repeated the incident. The first time they emergency responders had taken it lightly, but this time they had a serious talk with Herschel. They did give Herschel a fire helmet and a badge, but they also had a good heart-to-talk with him, and it never happened again.

Anna finally returned to one of her first loves, while they lived in Beaumont. She went to work for a florist there as the chief designer. For four years she made floral arrangements for people in the Beaumont area, using the knowledge she had gained while learning to be a Master Florist in Germany.

Herschel Senior worked a total of 38 years for Otis. After more than four years in Beaumont, they transferred him to Lake Charles, Louisiana in 1993. The family lived in Sulphur. It was not a particularly good move. Business was very slow. Otis started laying off people. Herschel had enough years in to have seniority, but because so many were laid off, he had to do a lot of fieldwork, servicing and inspecting along with his office duties.

Anna enrolled Herschel in a school for special children. She thought it would give her a break and some time to get interested in other things, but that was not to be. Herschel didn't like the school and he definitely did not like the teacher. He started throwing his shoes at her, and so almost every day, Anna would receive a call to come and get Herschel from school. The teacher was just not able to handle him.

Later, their family doctor suggested a group home where there were several young men like Herschel. The doctor pointed out that if anything were to happen to Senior and Anna, there would be no one to take care of Junior. Anna found it very difficult, but finally decided it was in Junior's best interest. The doctor made some calls and in September 1995, a group home in Jennings, Louisiana called and said they had an opening.

It was one of the most difficult days in Anna's life, the day the traveled to Jennings and left Herschel. He was twenty-two, but he had the mind of a three to four year-old. Anna said the most difficult part of leaving him there was that the home did not allow them to visit him for quite some time, so that he could adjust and make new friends at the home. This was very hard for Anna and Herschel, Senior.

During this time, Anna received more bad news. Her sister Johanna called and told her their mother had passed away on November 25, 1995.

For many years, Anna had been plagued with nerves whenever things were not going well, and this was no exception. Fortunately, this is where God, once again, stepped in and introduced her to some new friends.

Their next-door neighbor in Sulphur, a woman named Lana, attended Faith Temple church and she invited Anna to go with her, which she did. Once again, we see God's hand in placing the Lybargers right next door to someone who cared enough to invite Anna to church. Herschel was still feeling some uneasiness about church after the church in Houston had told them they did not dedicate babies when the family was not members. Therefore, he did not attend.

At the end of the service, when the pastor gave the invitation, Anna went forward. Choked up with emotion, she couldn't speak. Tears ran down her cheeks. She quickly found herself surrounded with new Christian friends, who laid their hands on her and prayed for her. She surrendered herself completely to God, and she said that almost instantly the cloud was lifted off her and she began to feel better.

The next day, they received a call from the group home telling them that young Herschel was doing great, and it was all right for them to come and visit him.

"What a reunion," Anna said. "God seemed to give us wings to fly to see him. We were amazed at how well he was doing. There were six other young men in the home and Herschel had made friends with all of them."

God continued to work and soon after joining there, Anna met Janice, who introduced her to her sister, Joyce Gant. They became very close friends. They both enjoy gardening. Anna said Janice and Joyce became true sisters in Christ. The family made Anna feel like she was one with them. Anna was very grateful to them and felt that this was a gift from God. Later, Joyce became quite ill and Anna spent a considerable amount of time in helping and caring for her. That friendship continues to this day.

In 1997, Anna decided that she was going to get on the fast track to becoming a citizen of the United States. She spent a year studying American History and American Government. On January 22, 1998 with her daughter Birgitta and her Christian friend Joyce at her side, Anna pledged allegiance to the United States and became a citizen. Tears of joy ran down her cheeks as they sang God Bless America. She said, "I thanked God for all the blessings I received over the years."

After a celebration dinner, they drove back to Sulphur and home.

Nineteen-ninety-eight was not a good year. Anna had to have gall bladder surgery, and before she got out of the hospital, the pressure from Herschel's job got to him and he suffered a heart attack. He had to have a quadruple bypass. Herschel and Anna were in the hospital at the same time across the ward from each other.

A year later, Herschel decided that the stress was not worth it, and he took early retirement from United Technologies, the company that took over Otis Elevators in 1976.The Lybargers packed up their goods and moved back to Texas.

Herschel's parents have a son-in-law who owns a large tract of land on FM 1097 West, a few miles northwest of Montgomery, Texas. Their home sits on a hill. Closer to the road are two brick homes. The elder Lybargers have lived in one of those homes for many years. The house next door to them has a small apartment built onto it, and that is where Anna and family moved temporarily. Across the road and a short distance to the northwest, is another home that needed some refurbishing. This is where Anna and Herschel spent their time for the next nine months, completely redoing this house built in the sixties. In December 1999, as soon as that was complete, Anna and Herschel moved there and have lived there for the past eleven years.

Seven months later, in July 2000, Anna had a heart attack and a double bypass.

Young Herschel spends most of the year at a facility for the handicapped in Louisiana. Several times a year, Anna drives there and brings him home. He spends, Easter, his birthday, Mother's Day, a week in the summer, Thanksgiving and Christmas with his family. The facility permits him to be away from there forty-five days a year, and Anna takes advantage of every one of those days.

Herschel seems to enjoy being at the home. He misses his friends when he visits the Lybargers. He is always ready to go back to Louisiana at the end of his visits.

Anna says that is a big relief to know he is happy there, but whenever she takes him back, she is in tears all the way back to Montgomery.

Herschel and his mother always pray together when he visits them. She taught him to pray, "Now I lay me down to sleep." He isn't able to put it in complete sentences, but hit the highlights, One night, not long ago, as she tucked him into bed, they prayed together. The television set was on and a football game was in progress. Herschel loves all kinds of sports. Anna turned the volume down and they began to pray. Herschel folded his hands and prayed, "lay down - -sleep - - keep- -I Lord - -" Then suddenly he hollered, "Touchdown, mom."

Anna had her eyes closed, and she had no idea, he was continuing to watch the game as he prayed. Anna said they both laughed, and she knows God has a sense of humor.

I have never seen a more devoted mother. Her comment to me was that she feels God gave her a special person to take care of. Herschel and Anna do their best to fulfill that duty, but it is all done out of love. She says she considers it an honor that God gave young Herschel to them as their son.

God blessed Anna by placing many people in her life, ones we have mentioned as we wrote this. These are people who cared for her and helped her during difficult times. Between them, Anna came to know Jesus on a personal basis and He has made a great difference in her life. She is now doing the same thing for young Herschel and many others. She is a devoted Christian, wife and mother.

She spends time every week caring for an elderly man suffering from Alzheimers. She goes to his home and provides care and encouragement for him. She also helps her in-laws who are quite elderly.

She is an inveterate cook. I have no idea how many jars of jam and jelly she makes in a year's time, but she seldom comes to Prayer Meeting without bringing jars of jam for someone. She also knows how to make around thirty different kinds of soup, which she generously shares. She provides chicken soup or some other delicacy when someone in the church family is ill.

Shortly after moving to the outskirts of Montgomery, the Lybargers joined New Beginnings Church, a very small church back in the woods a few miles from where they live. Anna said that after twenty-five years of prayer, Herschel forgave and forgot their unpleasant experience about the baby dedication, and came back to church on a regular basis. Unfortunately, the location of New Beginnings prevented them from ever becoming a thriving church. They finally closed the doors, because their membership was too small to support a pastor.

The Lybargers then joined his parents and other family, and became members of Benui Baptist Church. Anna sings with the group who provide special music and she also favors the congregation with Christian music played on her harmonica.

Herschel has some severe health problems. He suffers from scar tissue that has narrowed the passage of air into his lungs and as a result is on oxygen.. They are both faithful in attendance on Sunday mornings and Anna rarely misses the prayer service on Wednesday evenings.

Anna still likes flowers. She does the yard work at their home along with many other tasks. She and Herschel have a deep love for each other, for God and for our country. They celebrated their thirty-eighth wedding anniversary on August 12, 2010.

One of the many amazing things about Anna's life is her love for the United States. When she first came to this country, her love was still her home in Germany. She still remembered with some bitterness, the United States troops moving them from their apartment. Her marriage to a GI who was an alcoholic did not improve her feelings toward this country. Her second marriage to a jealous, uncaring man didn't help.

Somewhere along the line, as she became a strong believing Christian, the many people who befriended her, who loved her, and helped her, led her to make a dramatic change in attitude. She came to love this country and the freedom that comes with living here. In prayer meetings, she seldom fails to thank God for the United States and our freedoms.

She said, "I have made many mistakes, and have had some serious illness, but God keeps giving me a second chance. What more could I ask for? God has been so good to me. He has given me a loving home, a wonderful husband and family and a country that was built with love and provides freedom to worship God without having to be afraid to pray."

She recently wrote a poem that she read at church on July fourth. I have concluded this book with that poem. She is now a true patriot. She loves America, and what it stands for, and she gets very upset when she sees our leaders moving in a direction that threatens our freedoms. She has lived under the Nazis. She knows what it is like to have a totalitarian government dictate everything that you do. If only more Americans could sense that same concern.

In 1995, Anna's mother passed away peacefully in her sleep. Her sister Waltraud died in 2007.

One of Anna's sisters, Mathilde married a GI and lives in New York.

Anna went home once more in 2008. Her sister Johanna welcomed her, but at this point, Anna's home is really here.

Her daughter Birgitta lives in the Houston area and Anna enjoys their visits together. Son Jack also lives in Houston. He has suffered some of the same problems Anna did. His wife died of cancer when she was only thirty-eight. He is the father of a handicapped child, and has suffered through a divorce.

After many serious bouts with illness, Anna is a strong healthy woman, praising God for each day, and for living in the USA.

As we visited, she made a closing statement. If you have suffered some bumps and rough spots along the way, pay close attention to Anna's comments. God is the answer if we will only trust in Him.

"Today, I know that I could never live without God. Without Him, I would be nothing and nobody. The Christmas I spent in Germany with mother, my sister Johanna and her husband Hans was as if God had put the puzzle that we call life all together. The last few broken pieces I had still carried around inside of me were at that very moment mended back together without one scar left. Many times in the tribulations of my life, I had questioned God, 'Why me Lord? Lord you said that you would be with me all the way, and yet I have noticed that during the most troubled times in my life, when I needed you the most, you would seem to leave me.'

"That Christmas Eve, after everyone else had gone to bed, I walked out onto the balcony. The church bell across the street rang at two a.m.. Everything was dark and indeed it was a very silent night. The snow smelled so fresh and clean, and even in the dark, it glittered and sparkled more beautifully than ever. I leaned on the rails of the balcony and I prayed. I thanked God again for this wonderful Christmas He had given me – a Christmas I will remember as long as I live. I looked up toward Heaven, taking a deep breath, with my hands stretched out praising God and at that very moment He spoke to me.

"My child, my precious child, I love you and I have never left you, not even during your trials and sufferings. I have held you when you cried. My footprints were always there, right alongside you. It was then, that I carried you."

Anna said, "Suddenly, everything was clear in my mind. I knew from that moment on that God was always with me. For the first time, I even began to love myself, because God had created me just the way I was. "

AMERICA

America, created with beauty and grace,
By God Almighty-What a wonderful place
The foundation was laid many years ago
By proud and brave men, I think you should know

A land that was the land of the Pilgrim's pride
A land where our forefathers lived and died
They fought many battles in that sweet crystal air,
America, is a land beyond compare

Now is the time we all need to care
Freedom is something important to share
This country was born with freedom and love
The blessings were sent from way high above

Freedom to me is a dove in the sky
That has no limits where it can fly
I have experienced the other side as well
and let me tell you, it is nothing but hell

You have it all in the palm of your hand
You are a citizen of this beautiful land
How often do you sing that beautiful song
When deep down in your heart the feeling is wrong

I call upon all who love freedom, to stand
Let's sing God's praises and enjoy our land
America, America Stand proud and stand tall
A nation under God with liberty and justice for all

So honor your country and serve it with pride
Have courage and fight for the precious right
I just want you to know and hope you can see
That only in America will you truly be free.
By Anna Lybarger